Single Mom, Six Kids, & a Piano

THE EARLY YEARS

Paul Wesley La Canfora

Single Mom, Six Kids, & a Piano
Copyright © 2020 by Paul Wesley La Canfora

All rights reserved. No part of this book may be reproduced or transmitted in any form or by any means without written permission of the author.
    ISBN: 9798759330899
I have tried to recreate events and conversations from my memories of them. To maintain anonymity in some instances, I have changed individuals' names and identified details to protect their privacy.

Table of Contents

Prologue 5
Chapter 1 7
   He's Gone 7
Chapter 2 15
   The Move 15
Chapter 3 25
   Another Move 25
Chapter 4 35
   Burns and Stitches 35
Chapter 5 47
   Foxhole and Battle Plans 47
Chapter 6 57
   The Bad Men 57
Chapter 7 67
   Cindy the Snapping Pony 67
Chapter 8 73
   Oak Glen and Thurman Flat 73
Chapter 9 83
   The Bel-Air 83
Chapter 10 91
   Sara, the Talking Car 91
Chapter 11 104
   Lockheed Layoffs 104
Chapter 12 113
   What to Do? 113

Chapter 13 121
   To Banning, We Go! 121
Chapter 14 131
   Pioneer Town 131
Chapter 15 143
   The Red-Ryder BB Gun 143
Chapter 16 163
   Abuse of Power 163
Chapter 17 169
   Neighborhood Stories & Friends 169
Chapter 18 179
   Hard Decision 179
Chapter 19 189
   Love is Hard 189

Prologue

As time catches up in one's life, memories of yesteryear seem to present themselves more often. The most famous book in the world, the Holy Bible, says that our life is a vapor of smoke, meaning we are born, we live, and then we are gone. In our individual history, we create memories daily. Some may seem fleeting, but others appear as fresh as a favorite sunrise.

Throughout the centuries, kingdoms and races of people have risen and fallen. In some instances, only relics remain of their existence, such as the twenty-four thousand seat stadium in Ephesus or the great Pyramids.

There are many remnants of old logging cabins in the woods. Each piece of pottery or old rusty can tell a story of a life that someone took the time in their profession to gather and fashion the clay or melt iron to make metal. But who were they? What hopes and dreams of a good life did they hold? Did they marry and have children? What were their names, and what were their fortune or misgivings in life? Did they have faith in Jesus Christ or choose not to believe?

This makes me wonder. What will be said about my accomplishments or failures in life? What will be said about yours as well? So, by sharing a lifetime of memories, maybe, just maybe, something can be learned or laughed about. It could even be a miserable experience one can identify with, which could help others.

After sharing childhood memories with my children of being raised by a single mother, who led the way for her six children, they encouraged me to write these stories. With the help of my siblings, I tried to capture these experiences of certain periods of our childhood. So, maybe in the future, our children, relatives, or friends will want to remember these tiny glimpses of our cherished history that we call life.

I am the youngest of six children, known as the baby of the bunch. I wrote about some of these adventures from my humble perspective. So, if they seem to favor the views of the youngest child, well…there you go.

Growing up with a single mother was the time of our lives. It was incredibly adventurous, happy, sad, and hard but amusing. Virginia, my mother, was tough as nails, and her strengths were very honorable. She was a true woman to behold. Like any of us, she had her weaknesses. But her faith in God, fun spirit, tenacity to push forward and never give up, and deep love for her six children poured over into our lives. It was not easy for her and took a heavy toll on her health. But she persevered as hard as anyone to raise her six children.

One favorite quote my dear mother used on numerous occasions when money was tight—and often was— was, "Rob Peter to pay Paul."

In my youth, I thought it was an actual Bible verse for sure.

These events are based on a true story about Virginia and her six children. Despite being single, she fought hard to succeed and not lose her spark to raise and provide for her family. Her strengths and difficulties taught us much. This tale started in 1966.

Chapter 1

He's Gone

In 1966, the headline news was darkened with threats of war, drafts, and riots in the big cities. A few glimmers of good news surfaced, like Frank Sinatra recorded, *Strangers in the Night*. Luna 10, made by the Russians, orbited the moon, and the Beatles played their last live concert in Candle Stick Park, San Francisco.

In San Pedro, California, at the end of the hot summer month of July, Virginia's eyes opened quickly. "Oh no, it's time!"

Waddling from the chair, she headed straight for the phone and dialed the rotary. It seemed to ring for an eternity. Virginia remembered her husband's last words several nights before, "I may be in and out this week, or you won't see me at all. Work is going to be terribly busy. Long shifts…you know. Anyway, I need to get a pack of cigarettes, so I am going to leave now."

"Hello?" the groggy voice answered.

Frantically she said, "This is Virginia. I am so sorry to wake you. May I speak to my husband? I'm having my baby."

A long pause hung frightfully in the air. "I'm sorry, Virginia, he's no longer employed with us. He never called to let us know either way."

"When was the last time you've seen him?"

"It's been over a week. I'm sorry. Good luck to you."

Virginia dropped the phone and backed against the wall for support; a burning fear flushed her already aching body. Her suspicions had been confirmed. The marriage she once had was spiraling to a cataclysmic end. Every romantic thought of having her protector and provider by her side while having her sixth child flew out the window like a bad dream. Tears began to flow as her contractions quickly and painfully reminded her of the pressing need.

Dialing again with urgency, she had to wake her neighbor. She explained her great necessity for a babysitter and ride and apologized for waking them so late in the night. To her relief, they obliged.

The neighbor woman stayed with her five children as they slept. Each of them was born a year apart, except for this last child she was ready to deliver; he was a year and a half apart from the last.

This summer night was warm as she rushed out into the darkness. Slowly, she hobbled into the neighbor's idling car and shut the door. He nodded and slowly backed out of the drive, and away they went.

A panicked emptiness competed with her contractions. She dizzily watched the passing streetlamps as they headed to Little Saint Mary's Hospital. Between heavy breathing and painful contractions, Virginia tried to fathom her reality that her man was never coming back. Now, being alone with six children may be her fate—not to mention no money. Only spare change rustled around in her wallet.

A nurse met them at the emergency entrance and escorted Virginia to the delivery room. At 1:23 am, July 30th, the delivery of her over eight-pound baby took only forty-five minutes. She held her sixth child, glanced at the ceiling in a world of confusion, and fell asleep.

The next morning, she awoke. Looking around in that split second of dream-world and reality, she thought maybe her facing aloneness was just a nightmare. After seeing her hospital gown, reality crept back in. She slowly pushed herself up. Gazing out the first-floor window, deep emotions of a new and uncharted road in life shrouded her every thought. Reminiscing about how her marriage began to unravel, she drew a blank. *The last seven years of my life, I have been having babies. What could I have done? Now, I'm alone and need to take care of them and work?*

Her heart raced as she heard a tiny cry. Snapping back to why she was in the hospital, she saw her baby. He was bundled quietly in a small rolling crib the nurse wheeled in. Thoughts wove together of her other five children. *How will I feed them? How will I clothe them? How will I afford a home and a car to drive them to school? God, why is this happening to me?*

Tears flowed again as she heard a tap on the window. There, standing outside, was her husband. He motioned her in the way of asking, *where's the baby?*

A sparkle of hope returned. Virginia smiled slightly, reached over, and held up their child.

Coupling his hands on the glass to douse the rising sunlight, he smiled and waved.

She motioned for him to come in.

His smile fled, looking back at her. He waved one last time, then departed.

She glared hard out the window. *What is this? Why didn't he come in? He checked to see what room I was in and could only go to the window? Oh God, this is really happening. He is leaving me. He came just to see the baby. What about me? I bore his children.* Tears gushed down her cheeks as she sobbed.

Just then, the nurse walked in. "My dear, are you okay? What's the matter?" She inquired.

"No, no, I'm not okay. He's leaving me—I can't do it—I can't do it alone." She wept.

"What can't you do?" The nurse drew closer.

"I have six children. I can't raise them on my own. My God, my dear God, what do I do?"

"Don't worry, Virginia. I'll bring someone in who can help." The nurse quickly walked out the door while Virginia clutched the infant in her arms and stared at his tiny face.

Her mind envisioned this very same moment when her other children were born. All their lovely faces flashed through her heart and soul, but now, the difference with her last child, she was alone physically and mentally in the hospital. Her relatives all lived out of town.

Sitting back again and staring out the window with her baby in her arms, Virginia thought, *It's not supposed to be like this. My dreams were of a happy home until death do us part. God, this is my fault, isn't it? I don't know. What did I do wrong, and can I fix it?*

Looking again at the innocent face of her newborn son, she whispered, "I am sorry your father is not here for you, Pauly. I am so sorry, and—"

Just then, the door opened, and in walked the nurse and another nicely dressed woman. Half-rimmed reading glasses, held by a chain around her neck, were perched on the end of her nose. Her hair was a mix of streaks of gray and black. Holding a folder under her left arm, she said, "You must be…Virginia Susan La Canfora, I presume?"

Wiping her tears and straightening her golden blonde hair, Virginia replied, "Yes, that's me."

"I am a social worker, and I'm here to offer you help. You see, we offer a wonderful placement program for those children whose families can't cope…of course. This program is for people like you who are in need. It promises that all your children will be placed in nice homes if you so choose. Once we have your approval, we can enter their names and begin the process. This way, you can have the freedom to get your life in order and not have to worry about the burden your children pose. The sooner we do this, the sooner you can get back on your feet." The worker smirked and awaited an answer.

Feet. Get back on my feet? My husband just left me. What is she saying?

A rage began to swirl like a hurricane, a fury ignited by the foreign words: "Your children will have nice homes." *Foster care? What?*

She felt like a mama bear. Now was the time to growl and claw at those words and to clear out her den of this unwelcome offer. *No one is taking any of my children!*

A reality slap across her face instantly cleared Virginia's thinking. Putting on a front and hiding the swelling rage inside, she smiled at the lady and said, "Thank you, I will have to think about it."

The social worker returned the smile and said, "Well, please consider the proposition. But don't wait too long with your decision. These things do happen…and we offer you our services. I will be back in a while so we can speak further." She moved closer, looked at her infant, and said, "You have a wonderful little baby boy."

The social worker turned, and she and the nurse exited and shut the door.

Virginia thought, *Can things possibly get any worse?*

Looking at her child and replaying the strange offer to give her children away swirled like a worse nightmare than having her husband leave her. A devastating sadness draped her heart as she stared at her baby.

She calmed down and prayed. "Lord Jesus, you have been with me my whole life. You have answered my prayers every step of the way, even in the toughest times, like when my father died. Now, please help me again. What do I do? Please forgive me if I caused this. Please give me the strength to take the next step. My insides are burning, and my heart is crushed. I don't know what to do. I have no money, no food in our cabinets, we're behind on rent, and I don't know where to go…but you do. Please, please help me."

A sudden thought encircled her. Acting on impulse, Virginia slowly got out of bed. She approached the closet and grabbed her clothes. *If I show signs of a nervous breakdown, they'll think I have cracked and take my children from me. I got to get out of here.*

Quietly getting dressed and combing her hair the best she could, she stepped back into the room and bundled her baby. As she stared out the window, she saw a pathway leading to the street.

Taking a deep breath, she slowly opened the door to the hall and felt all eyes were upon her. She stared down the long stretch at the nurse's station; they appeared busy.

To Virginia's relief, as she looked around the door, she saw that the emergency exit was a short distance away. Smoothly, she stood tall and tried to look as casual as possible even though she had just given birth hours before. She slipped out the door and shut it quietly. The hall seemed to stretch on as she walked to the emergency exit.

Her adrenaline surged as she screamed on the inside, *Hurry up, Virginia!*

Opening the door to her escape, she dared not turn to see if eyes were upon her. The warm summer morning wrapped around them as her heart thumped and raced. It felt as if she was escaping a prison.

Guilt began to run through her mind. *Should I be doing this? Is my baby going to be all right? How much do I owe the hospital? I'm just walking out, and worse, what if they come to my home and track me down? God, what am I doing?*

Heavy emotions chilled her body, and she felt dizzy.

Heading for the boulevard, she thought it was her best chance to find a pay phone. The buildings seemed a blur, and beside one store was the phone booth. She stepped inside and searched for change to make a call. It felt like a herd of nurses would be out frantically looking for her.

The phone rang, and her neighbor answered and was obliged to come to get her again. She stayed in the shadows for what seemed forever, a block away, out of view of the hospital. Finally, her ride appeared, and she quickly got in the car, and he drove her home.

"Just curious," her neighbor asked, "why am I picking up a woman who just delivered a baby a block or so away from the hospital?"

Beads of sweat formed on her forehead, and her mouth turned to cotton as she swallowed. "I, um…would rather not answer that if you don't mind."

He nodded and said, "Then your secret is safe with me."

He looked over and smiled. His elderly wrinkles pushed up his sparkling eyes.

~

Inside the hospital, the nurse held a breakfast tray. "Here you go, Virginia, I have your…"

She stepped in, set the food on the tray, then noticed the baby was gone and the bathroom door was shut. Tapping on the door, she called, "Virginia, are you in there?"

No answer came, and she opened the door to an empty room. "Maybe she's strolling around."

The nurse stepped into the hall and searched the corridors on every floor. She even looked outside, but Virginia was nowhere to be seen.

The nurse checked at the desk. "Did we release Virginia? She was in that room there," she said, pointing down the hall.

The clerk behind the counter checked her forms. "No, not according to our records."

The nurse looked back at the room and paused. "I wonder if we scared her?"

The clerk asked, "Scared who?"

The nurse shook her head and said, "Nothing, never mind."

She headed back into the room, opened the closet, and saw that Virginia's belongings were gone. The only thing neatly hanging up was her hospital gown.

~

Stepping out of the car, Virginia realized how much her body ached. She was quickly welcomed by her covey of children hugging her leg, eager to see their new addition. They had not a care in the world about the change ready to happen. So oblivious to the more significant concern of the tidal wave crashing upon them.

Her neighbor informed her that her husband had come home in the early morning, packed his things, and left. The neighbor wondered if he was going on an extended business trip.

Virginia gave many thanks for her neighbor's blessings of help. She went inside and hugged her children.

After the gaggle of little questions, she smiled and fed her children lunch with what little food they had.

Her oldest child Maureen asked where their father was going. "He was quiet, Mommy but gave each of us a hug before he left."

Virginia didn't know what to say but only smiled.

Finally, she sat down and realized the shots of pain around her mid-section were overwhelming. *Ouch, I just gave birth and should be resting.*

Well, at least Pauly was easy since I've had a lot of practice. She strangely amused herself.

Looking around at the small collection of furnishings, oddities, and paintings on the wall, she thought, *I can't afford rent, and we are behind.*

As the children played outside, she changed the toddler's diapers, fed her baby, and took a few solitude moments to think of what to do.

The phone rang a few times, but she dared not answer it. *Maybe it's the hospital? I'd better call mom; we can't stay here.*

After the unpleasant call and the reminder from her mother that she shouldn't have married that man, they agreed the wise move would be to move closer to the small town of Yucaipa.

A few days later, after packing her suitcase and collecting a few photo albums, Virginia waited outside. She watched as her brother arrived with his pickup. There, standing on the sidewalk, was Virginia, her six children, a few suitcases, and the upright Betsy Ross piano.

"Seriously, Virginia, you must be ape thinking I'm loading the heaviest piece of furniture?" her brother protested.

"Really, Lloyd, I'm ape? That's a musical instrument we all took lessons on when we were kids. It's for my children. It's coming with us!" she demanded. "My neighbors will help load it. They at least brought it this close."

"All right, all right, keep a cool head. It's making the trip."

Mumbling and grumbling, Lloyd managed, with the help of a neighbor, to strap the piano to the bed of the pickup truck.

After loading her few belongings, they all squeezed into the single cab with some of the children on her lap. She looked at the house one more time. A sickening lump upset her stomach as she thought about the paintings, furniture, and knick-knacks she had to leave behind. All memories that the two collected over the seven years of marriage were sitting alone in the empty house. Gone was the laughter and gone were the dreams they had together. But one thing was for sure; a new chapter was beginning.

Chapter 2

The Move

Virginia, her six children, suitcases, and an old Betsy Ross upright piano were in the truck. Ready or not, another life far from this one was beginning.

Maureen-six years old; Patrick-five, Greg-four, Cynthia-three; Keith was almost two; Paul, the newborn baby, and their mother headed onto the moderate freeway, the warm summer blowing through the wind wing. Virginia looked at her children's eager faces as they cruised on the ninety-one through the sprawl.

They left the San Pedro concrete jungle behind as they made their way through the lonesome dry canyons of Corona. Soon, the San Jacinto's blue range slowly soared into view. Virginia was familiar with the drive from visiting her mom when time and money allowed.

Enormous wonder ruled her mind about what to do next and how to provide. Waves of fear made her heart pound, but she concealed it well, always praying silently.

When they merged east on the ten freeway, her eyes glanced north to the R marked into the hillside by the students at the University around 1915, which indicated they had indeed reached Redlands.

Passing the vast orange groves and protruding wind turbines, Virginia saw the trees were standing perfectly in rows with too many to count. Faint scents of old smudge-pot oil and orange blossoms whiffed through the cab. Finally, the approaching San Gorgonio range capped the adventure.

They pulled off onto the long Yucaipa boulevard. With the San Bernardino peaks slightly northeast and impending foothills ahead, the two-lane road led past more orange groves planted along the base of the Crafton Hills.

Looking past Oak Glen Rd, she spied the small fruit stand hoping to return for fresh vegetables.

The passing gear kicked in as her brother revved up to motor for the steep climb up Chicken Hill, which led to the upper shelf of Yucaipa. The thin boulevard ran up to the base of the foothills to a quaint little park called Flag Hill. But for them, they turned right, reaching 4th street and heading to Avenue B. Virginia's heart was glad to see a local grocery store. Food Fair was across the street. She didn't own a car and was already planning how far of a walk it would be to the local wares.

Lloyd pulled into the driveway of a small rental he and her mom procured for her and unloaded what few things they had. Much to their happiness, the air was noticeably cooler there than in the valley.

The older children ran through the tiny empty house, proclaiming where they would sleep.

"I have a surprise for you, Virginia." Her brother waved her inside.

She stepped into the kitchen and teared up at the sight of a refrigerator.

Virginia hugged her brother and said, "Thank you, Lloyd. How did you do all of this so quickly?"

"Thanks, but it came with the place."

When she opened the fridge, it was full of food, milk, butter, and a bottle of orange juice, to her second surprise.

"This is what we supplied. You just keep those little mouths fed, okay, sis?"

"What a wonderful gift. I can pay you back somehow. It may take a while," Virginia said as she wiped her tears away.

Lloyd bellowed, "Hey kids, you like your new house?"

The older four children giggled and wrapped around his legs, forbidding him to walk.

"You boys take care of your mother, you hear me? You are the men of the house. You need to protect and help her. Don't whine or gripe. She has a lot of work to do."

The boys nodded in agreement as their uncle rubbed their blond heads.

After muscling the piano into the house, Lloyd said his goodbyes.

Virginia looked at the barren house and wondered where and how she could acquire furniture. With the children running in and out, she stepped to the piano. Flipping up the wooden cover, she slowly touched a few ivory keys. The high tones echoed off the hard walls and wood floors.

An immediate connection between her and the instrument was struck. *I feel like you ole piano. Full of music and cheer. But alone, no one knows what kind of music is inside. You're sitting here every day waiting for someone to come to you and bring out all beautiful and hidden melodies. Yep, ole Betsy, you and I are just alike.*

Over the next few months, word spread throughout the small neighborhood and church about a single mom with a load of kids. Some generosity arrived in the form of limited used furnishings, dishes, utensils, and a few toys.

Sitting on the porch while the older kids played and the younger was napping, she pulled out the Blue-Chip stamp catalog. She perused the pages as a large toy caught her eye. Counting and recounting her stamps, she grinned. Soon, a small battle of guilt arose as she looked back at the bent pages keeping a place of much-needed kitchen items she desperately was saving for. "Oh Virginia, you can survive without these things a bit longer," she whispered as she realized that these decisions were becoming routine.

What can I live without, what can I borrow, and how do I become fluent in robbing Peter to pay Paul?

She placed the guilty envelope in the mail a few weeks later, and the long-awaited prize arrived.

The postman smiled as he set the large box down. "Do you need any help, ma'am?"

She said no, and the older children felt a rush of the Christmas spirit since it was around the corner.

Hollering and leaping with excitement, "What is it?" they yelled in unison from the inquisitive minds.

"Not now. It's for Christmas. You'll have to wait."

Virginia set the large box in the corner of the tiny garage, and the two older boys were delighted. They tried to imagine what could be in there.

"Could it be a tree fort? Maybe an army tank?"

Even Maureen, the oldest, wondered, "What if it was a snow cone maker?"

Cynthia liked all ideas and just wanted to open the present.

The endless dreams bounced off the tiny garage walls as they stared at the box until, slowly, Virginia lowered the small garage door. And there it would remain until Christmas.

Lying in bed each night, the thoughts of the box swirled. Greg asked Patrick, "What do you think it is?"

"It's a pirate ship!" Patrick smiled.

"That's a small ship. Maybe it needs putting together. That'd be cool?"

Leaping up in bed, they had a vision of sword fights. Next, they hoisted the Jolly Rodger flag. Their dream bubbles exploded with excitement until sleep pushed their weary eyes closed.

The day arrived when Maureen tapped on their door and said, "Merry Christmas, time to wake up?"

The children shot out of bed and dashed to the living room where the humble tree stood. Gazing at the wrapped large box, it seemed to glisten with dazzling colors and screamed to be torn open.

The four children crawled up next to it, oblivious to the few smaller presents in their surroundings. Time was fleeting by as heads glanced for mom's green light. But she had first to change the two younger boys' diapers. As the clock ticked, she had to warm milk by heating water on the stove. Next, she dipped the full Pyrex bottles in the pot and brought them to temperature.

Keith waddled up with a bottle in his mouth and a blanket over his shoulder. He stared at his siblings and saw how they were sitting. He mimicked them and sat.

Cynthia hugged him and pointed to the pretty things on the tree. "Look, Keith...look at all the pretty decorations of our Christmas tree."

Keith pulled the bottle out, pointed, and said, "Chee."

Squeezing him tightly, Cynthia laughed. "Yes, tree. You are so smart."

Keith smiled again and said, "Smaut."

He shoved the bottle back in for a long drink of warm milk.

Virginia finally sat down with the baby, Paul, in her lap. He laid across her arms with his bottle and slurped away, oblivious to hovering excitement. "Kids, we have much to be thankful for, and you have all been terrific. I thank God He has provided for us with a home, food, clothing, and each other." A pause hung as her eyes filled with tears. "Merry Christmas. I love all my children. Now, who wants to open presents?"

She knew there wasn't much under the tree. She arranged the few presents to look like many. She cleverly rewrapped baby food and bottles she already owned for the youngest two. She knew they wouldn't notice a thing. "Now, you four get to unwrap the box together., Everyone sharing and doing it at the same time. Ready, set, go!"

They jumped at the package like several chainsaws; the paper flew in the air exposing the familiar cardboard. The top, held securely shut by thick tape, was also lined with heavy staples.

"Patrick, you may get a butter knife. Walk, don't run."

In a flash, Patrick cut the tape while they kept trying to get a glimpse into the box.

"What's in there?" Greg yelled as Maureen began to pull at the staples.

Cynthia cried, "Hey, you're blocking me!" She cleverly slid around, squeezing between the tree and the box.

Keith was lying on his back, cuddled in his blanket, draining his bottle, and staring at the ceiling.

Suddenly, there was a pop! Maureen managed the first staple free. She instructed her brothers to pull on the others until, *pop, pop, pop!* One by one, the staples were now useless and no longer a barrier to their progress.

They smiled as they slowly opened the gift. Their eyes were wide as the reflection of red paint shined from the morning sun and the few Christmas lights. Staring into the box, the children giggled as they revealed the mysterious present. A bright red steel wagon screaming to be let loose for immediate adventures.

They stared and touched the new and finely shaped bed.

Patrick gripped the handle and smiled. "Mom, this is far out, thank you!"

Ripping the box open, they pulled the large wagon onto the hardwood floor and jumped into it. Maureen envisioned herself giving rides to her baby brothers and sister. At the same time, the older boys imagined flames and tire smoke from the green light of a drag strip.

The few other gifts were opened in a split second, but all seemed to bow to the mighty red wagon. All eyes kept merging back to the shiny paint. Something brand new was theirs. They had become used to hand-me-downs. The first Christmas far from their first home was exceptional.

Virginia's time was brief as she tended to breakfast of pancakes and Karo syrup for the troops.

After lunch, grandma arrived and bore more gifts. The kids exploded once again with double excitement.

"I don't know how you do it, Virginia. My grandchildren have enough energy to light an entire city."

"Yeah, they drain it out of me first."

They laughed.

"Well, you know the saying…any cow can have a calf. But it's how you raise them."

"Thanks, Mom. I don't know if that's a compliment or not. Assuming I'm the heifer?"

Grandma laughed. "No, no, it's about how you raise your children. Silly, you're not a heifer by any means."

Virginia smiled as they conversed, and each opened one more gift.

Soon, dinner was served, and like most exciting days, it ended. Grandma departed, and it was time for bed.

Patrick and Greg were playing with toys in the dark. Cynthia and Maureen were asleep, along with the two babies.

Virginia sat and stared at the tree alone. Gathering her thoughts, sudden memories of her father, who passed away many years earlier, came to mind.

Joe was always thoughtful of his children. He was a navy man who served twenty years and survived several WWII battles, including Midway and the Pacific skirmishes. He served on four of the first five carriers and ended his service aboard the USS Enterprise.

She closed her eyes and thought of the Christmas letter she had written to him in second grade when he was off to war. Missing him so, in that year he was engaged in battle, she begged her mom to leave Christmas up for him until he returned. This was her prayer that he returned from the war, which was answered. She missed his comforting laugh and silly jokes, but most of all, she just wanted to hear his voice one more time, telling her, "It will be okay."

Virginia felt very alone as the lights on the tree glistened through her tears. She sobbed heavily. Her many wonderings about how this new life would be and how she would ever provide were suddenly replaced with a glimmer of hope and peace.

"God, thank you." Making the sign of the cross, she prayed, "Our Father, Who art in heaven, hallowed be Thy name. Thy kingdom come, Thy will be done, on earth as it is in heaven…" She paused, staring at the tree as tears still streamed. She continued, "…who trespass against us. Lead us not into temptation but deliver us from evil…Amen."

She whispered, "It's going to be okay, Virginia."

Sitting in the armchair with a new blanket her mother gave her wrapped around her legs, she fell asleep.

~

The light outside slowly crept up to start the new day, and a slight clunking woke her. There, below the tree, were Patrick and Greg. They had set up their green plastic army men and quietly prepared for battle. Suddenly, she heard a faint cry from the basket as the baby was hungry.

The day pressed on, and the older kids took to the red wagon like a new car and quickly incorporated it into front and backyard transportation. Then, out in the big world, to the street. The avenue was dead-end and uphill. Soon the wagon was wheeled up a little way as they piled in, and the race began.

Virginia yelled out the window, "Be careful, and watch for cars!"

Oblivious to the announcement, they pushed the wagon up and down the street, and soon curtains opened. Liveliness seemed to wake the quiet neighborhood with the steady sound of children's laughter.

A neighbor boy who was Patrick's age came out to play, and soon, the boys took to military games. They set up the army men and knocked them down until Jay, the neighbor, said, "Let's pretend we're cowboys, and there are rustlers afoot."

Greg looked down at his feet. "What does that mean?"

"We will show you." Jay ran home and returned with a long rope. "We're the cowboys, and you're trying to steal our horses."

Greg ran as Jay yelled, "Get the rustler. He's stealing our horses! Quickly, we need to string him up!"

Patrick grabbed Greg, and they tied Greg to the Walnut tree in the front yard. Much to Greg's protest.

"I don't want to play this game…besides, you're the bad guys!" Greg squirmed.

"Pipe down, you rustler. You'll have to hang!" Jay sneered as they secured the knot. "Now, Patrick, let's go alert the sheriff that we caught the thief!"

Patrick nodded, and they took off to the backyard.

They became distracted, and Jay's mom yelled for him to come home.

Patrick arrived through the backdoor and said, "Is lunch ready? I'm hungry. I want peanut butter and jelly!"

"What did you say?" Virginia stopped and stared.

"Oh…may I please have a peanut butter and jelly sandwich?"

"That's better. Always mind your manners. Never burst in demanding something…ever!"

She turned and heard a faint cry. "Where's Greg? Wasn't he playing with you?"

Patrick's eyes widened as Maureen and Cynthia looked out the front window and saw the crier.

"Why's Greg tied to the tree?" Maureen asked.

Virginia rushed to the window and yelled, "Patrick!"

So were the memorable days on Ave B.

Chapter 3

Another Move

The year was 1967, and the Vietnam War was in full swing. Elvis and Priscilla were married, and civil unrest was in the big cities as riots erupted in Detroit. Toy cosmonauts were sold in the USSR while tragedy struck the USA space program. One of the Apollo capsules suffered a horrible fire killing the three astronauts on board.

The popular musical band called, The Monkees released their second album. While the headlines portrayed turbulent times, Virginia worried for her children. She tried not to let them see the local news. But sometimes, leaving the small black and white television on while dealing with the babies, the older siblings often caught sight of war coverage.

"Patrick and Maureen, turn that off." Virginia would march in front of their curious eyes and click the knob. "Get outside and play!"

After weighing employment options and being afraid to seek assistance after the great hospital escape, Virginia cautiously contacted a social worker. But this time on her own terms.

She was not interested in the foster care system but desperately needed financial aid. The worker arrived that very week and listened to her concerns.

The nice lady stated, "Virginia, in four to five years, your youngest child will enter school. We highly suggest that you stay home. You can let the welfare system assist you. You know the best thing for your children is you being with them. So, when your last child enters school, that's the time you should be working."

"Look, I am not new to motherhood. I deeply recognize they need me. So, thank you. I don't need to be reminded of that. Now, being given money I didn't earn goes against everything I've been taught. I was raised on the belief to provide for myself and be beholden to no one." Virginia sighed.

"Yes, but your situation is precisely what this program is designed for. Don't feel ashamed. You can stay on Welfare your entire life," the visitor added.

"I'm a World War II brat. I can't help it. It's taking from others and giving it to me is what is so bothersome. If I go on welfare, then I'll sure work hard to get off it. That day will be a great day in this household, and it gives me a goal to fight for. I don't want to burden or be beholden to anyone at any time. This entire ordeal has tried me more than anyone knows. I can't stand owing people anything."

"Well, Virginia, maybe that day will come. You have some decisions to make. Let us know what you would like to do."

After the social worker departed, Virginia pondered the idea of taking something that was not hers, which was intensely troublesome.

A week later, after praying and discussing with her mom, they agreed it would be the best course. The financial aid offered through the welfare system was very little. Adding up the bills and counting what was past due, Virginia shook her head and wondered how to stretch her dollar. She thought of the commodity lines she would have to stand in for a monthly supply of goods.

"I am really going to need to swallow my pride. Food lines, good gracious, has it really come to this?"

Staring out into the front yard, she watched her children play in the wagon and whispered, "I can only imagine what's in the food boxes. Well, Virginia, you're going to have to get really creative with your cooking…and be thankful."

A few days later, Grandma called. Frankie was her name. And strange as it may seem, when she was born, her father had desperately wanted a boy. So, he named her Frankie.

The children thought her name was cool, and the younger gave it little thought.

Frankie had a rough upbringing. Born in 1908, her family split when she was very young. At the age of three, since she was not a prized son, which her alcoholic father wanted, she was given over to her grandparents, who were farmers and sharecroppers.

Frankie said, "Virginia, I need to move to Alabama because work is wanting me to finish my years of employment there and retire. I will be gone for three to four years. It's fine with me because I'll be able to visit some aging relatives. So, if you would like to move into my house until I return, it's all yours, rent-free. Now the kids will have room to stretch their legs."

Virginia stared as the words sank in. She thought, *What a break, I'll be able to manage food on the table and clothes for the kids. God in Heaven, I won't have to pay rent. This is good news.*

Tears formed as she said, "Thank you so much, really! I'll take care of the house, and if anything gets broken, which I think we can count on it, I'll repair it. We'll do our best to keep it clean, and when you return, it will be like you never left."

"Well, Virginia, I know you'll do your best. Now, all you have to do is get an automobile."

Automobile, I'm just trying to survive, I can't think of trying to buy a car. "Yes, maybe someday soon. I can't imagine owning one now. It would just sit and collect dust. I can't afford even a drop of gas."

For some reason, this strangely brought laughter.

"Virginia, you keep doing what you are doing. I think you will make it after all."

They said their goodbyes, and Virginia called for a family meeting and told the ecstatic kids the good news. With many cheers, they wanted to depart that very hour, but they had to wait. With this new move into grandma's home on Avenue E, Virginia's excitement peaked because the house rested on the back of a half-acre of land. Grandma's house was a bit larger but had only two bedrooms. With the trials of their sleeping arrangement in this current home already, she thought, *Well, I will deal with it when we get there, one day at a time, Virginia, one day at a time.*

This would be a challenge to pack in her many children, especially as they grew. But with the huge yard, it was a dream come true.

Before she knew it, her brother Llyod was over, and they packed up the truck. And once again, he was grumbling about moving the old Betsy Ross upright. "Really, I need to tote this dumb piano again?"

"That dumb ole piano I will never depart with. I'll help."

"Take it easy, sis. I'm only complaining. I will ask your neighbor for help again."

They loaded up and pulled away from the fond little house, and just a few minutes later, they arrived at their new home. Grandma's driveway came into view, and their uncle steered his truck up the long center drive.

The house was set on the very back of the lot, which made the land seem endless to the children. According to their grins, it felt as if they were entering royalty. The older boys saw the potential for adventure because of the massive yard. They had visited a few times before. It was easier for grandma to drive to their house since they did not own a car.

Virginia's routine at the Ave B house was to load the youngest two boys in the wagon, and the other four would carefully pull them across the street to Food Fair. She would lead, and the kids would pull the wagon. Each would guide the younger. Now, the store would be over a mile away.

"Hmm, well, we will all just have to exercise a little more," Virginia said. Making a quick decision had become a custom as well.

The day was bright, and moving into the new home quickly took shape since she didn't have much. Inside, the four walls seemed spacious. Virginia was intrigued by the older boy's idea to please set up their beds in the enclosed covered breezeway, and they couldn't contain their excitement. They jumped up and down to press their mom's will their way.

She thought, *Brilliant idea, boys, this will solve my worries.* "Follow me, and I will call out the sleeping arrangements."

They lined up behind her as she led them through the house. "This bedroom on the right is for Maureen and Cynthia." She pointed to the other room and said, "This is where you boys will sleep, and Keith will join you. Paul's crib will be with the girls and me. Patrick and Greg, I like your idea about using the breezeway. Let's wait until you are a little older, but not now."

"Ah, Mom, please?" They protested, and she stood her ground.

"Not yet, and that is final." She crossed her arms, which meant she was serious, and there would be no more speaking about the matter.

The kids learned when Mom could be persuaded and when they pushed her too far. Crossing her arms meant she won the battle, and anything else that followed was folly.

Speaking of declaring spaces, as the kids grew older, it became customary for the six kids to claim their ever-so-important domain. It could be a space in the bedroom or a favorite seat at the dinner table. It didn't stop there. Even in front of the television was fought for. Among the six kids, this was always a battle worth fighting for; you get the point.

So, the two girls and four boys had their sleeping assignments etched in stone.

Maureen, the oldest, asked, "Mom, where are you going to sleep?"

Virginia smiled and pointed to the large window in the living room. "I will put my dresser in your room, and I will leave my bed for Cynthia. That way, some nights, I will join her, and others, I will sleep on the couch."

"But do you want to trade?" Maureen said, concerned. "I can sleep on the couch if you need me to."

"No, thank you, I want my two girls to have the best room." She smiled.

In Virginia's heart, feeling this choice was the best thing to do for her children, selflessly giving the best accommodations and comfort to her kids instead of her. This also became her custom.

Maureen said, "Mom, I…" She ran into her arms and squeezed. "I love you."

"I love you too, Maureen. You girls enjoy your room."

They scurried inside and giggled with excitement. It was a tiny space, but it seemed larger than life, and they felt rich.

The younger boys were too young to remember. Keith was old enough to shed diapers and skilled at walking. His vocabulary was growing as well. He was always watching and learning from the older kids.

Their beds were set up, mattresses plopped down, and the few furnishings were set in place. It appeared this was a massive break for the family.

Virginia looked around at the roomy house, the galley kitchen, and the enormous yard and smiled. With quiet ease in her heart, she felt that God heard and answered her prayer. From not knowing where to go and what to do, after seven months since the birth of her last child, she felt a more definite plan lay ahead. *Thank you, Lord Jesus. I know, one day at a time, Virginia, one day at a time,* she prayed.

After a week of settling in, the outdoors called Patrick and Greg. They needed to attend to the important job of mini road sculpting and ditch-digging for their Matchbox, Hot Wheels cars, and a bag of green plastic army men.

On the east side of the front yard was a small dirt elevation. They took to their kid duties at lightning speed as they pulled grandpa's old bucket and shovels from the garage. Soon, a small metropolis was developed.

Patrick and Greg had no problem with creativity and ideas. They built roads and then filled the bucket with water for the storm. They turned their project into a giant flood zone which decimated their labor. The torrent destroyed the roads with added sound effects and explosions, and the cars careened down the waterway.

"Let's build it again!" Patrick yelled. "I have a cool idea. This time, let's build a lake on top, then we will fill it and break the dam."

Greg chimed in, "Oh, you said a bad word!"

With laughter, they engaged in the engineering of the lake.

Maureen was not into having dirt under her nails or grass stains on her clothes like the boys. She thought of grown-up things like music and stayed close to help Mom.

She stepped outside and asked Cynthia, "Do you want to walk around the entire yard with me?"

"Sure, ain't no use sitting around doing nothing." Cynthia stood.

"Let's go then, and ain't is not a word," Maureen corrected.

With excitement, they set out on their quest. They started at the boy's construction site. Maureen questioned them if they liked the new yard. They all agreed it was the best and largest ever. Then the girls looked down and admired the realistic roads and lake.

Cynthia, distracted from her course, quickly jumped into the dirt and mud. "This is far out, what you built. Can I dig a road?"

Maureen interrupted, "Cynthia, I invited you on a walk."

Staring hard at the mud, toys, and digging tools, she said, "Oh, all right."

Cynthia stood, said goodbye to her brothers, and continued following the fence-line south.

They could see through the chain link and hedges into another backyard. It was well-groomed and sprinkled with fruit trees of orange and tangerines. A small birdbath rested at the end of the walkway.

Each picked up a stick and ran them across the fence, clicking and humming as they went. They saw a small lawn and a concrete walkway to the mailbox through the fence as they approached the neighbor's front yard.

"Hello, girls." A friendly voice rang out.

Maureen smiled at the elderly lady wearing a grayish bun hairstyle and a dark floral dress. She was seated on her front porch chair. "Good morning," she replied.

"Frankie said her grandchildren were moving in. I am Mrs. Burrow. My pleasure to meet you."

"I'm Cynthia!" she shouted.

"Manners, Cynthia," Maureen said sternly.

Smiling at their new neighbor, she said, "We are glad to meet you. My name is Maureen, and I am the oldest. This is my baby sister, Cynthia."

Cynthia frowned.

"Well, my dears, glad to meet you. Come over here. I have something for your mother." She stood and went inside.

Cynthia looked up at Maureen for approval, and Maureen nodded, and they set off.

They walked past the fence and up to the neighbor's front porch. The girls knew it was forbidden to touch another's property, especially to enter anyone's house without permission. They stood quietly, curious as to what the item would be.

Pushing the squeaky screen door, Mrs. Burrow returned, holding a small cardboard box filled with fruit from her backyard.

Maureen grinned. "Thank you very much. Our mother loves fruit."

Surprisingly, their nice neighbor held out her hand, and there were two butterscotch candies in her palm. "And these are for you two, very polite young ladies."

Again, Cynthia looked up at Maureen for approval, and Maureen nodded.

Both girls were happy and accepted the gifts. And after a small chit-chat, they said goodbye.

As they stepped into their front yard, Cynthia said, "She's a nice lady, ain't she?"

"Yes, she is, and once again, ain't is not a word. Come on, let's finish our walk around the yard. It's not too far, and I will carry the fruit."

They headed to the west side of the lot and passed over the driveway. They heard a strange humming sound from the other neighbor's garage as they approached. The large door was open, and the closer they came, the louder the sound.

Maureen and Cynthia arrived at the fence. There they could see shelves full of rocks. Some were beautiful and round. Others were square, polished, and natural rocks. Various colors adorned the displays; they had never seen anything like it.

They caught a glimpse of an elderly man wearing brown pants and a shirt. He walked around the machines and then disappeared. From what they could see, his workshop seemed tidy.

Maureen shrugged and headed up the fence line. The rest was blocked by a row of hedges that led to the westside neighbor's house. That house was strangely set back from the rock machine house. At the end of the fence by the corner of the backyard, an older pony greeted them. It snorted a few feet away.

"He looks scary," Cynthia said, stepping back.

"He...is a she. Mom says her name is Cindy, and she bites." Maureen stepped away.

"Wow, they must be rich to own a horse." Cynthia skipped behind.

"Maybe, but Cindy's a pony, not a horse," Maureen corrected.

Stopping and frowning, Cynthia said, "What's the difference? They all look like horses to me."

They arrived home, pushed through the back slider door, and headed for the kitchen. The girls showed their mom the gift, and she was elated. Patrick and Greg burst in, curious about what could be in the box. They were let down when they only saw fruit.

"The nice lady gave me and Maureen butterscotch candy," Cynthia bragged.

"Awe, lucky. Can we go over and ask for candy?" Greg inquired.

Virginia said, "Heavens no, Greg. You can't just waltz over and ask someone for candy. That's rude. You need to be invited, and if they offer you a treat, you may have some."

While Virginia focused on the fruit, Cynthia stuck her tongue out at Greg.

"Mom, Cynthia's sticking her tongue out at me!"

"Did not!" Cynthia quickly said as she performed a disappearing act out of the room.

"Kids! Go play, or I will find some chores for you!"

Like scurrying mice, they fled in every direction.

"Mom?" Maureen said. "Mrs. Burrow is very nice."

"Yes, she is. Grandma introduced us a while back. I would like to visit her if I ever get a free moment. But it's cooking, laundry, endless vacuuming, and dishes. Not to mention diapers that keep me busy twenty-four-seven."

"Can I help with anything?" Maureen looked up with a smile.

"Thanks. Can you please wash the fruit, and we will put some in the bowl and the rest in the fridge."

They chatted about music and shopping as they prepared lunch to feed the army.

"How do you like living here?" Virginia asked.

Maureen's eyes widened. "I love it. The yard is so big, and I like the long driveway. Our neighbor on the right has a bunch of neat rocks and a loud machine. Do you know what it is?"

"It's a rock tumbler. He polishes and cuts them. It brings out their inner beauty."

"That sounds neat. I would like to see them up close."

"I have met him as well; they are the Wheelers. They are retired, and that is his hobby. His garage is full of shelf after shelf of rocks. I don't know what he does with them all, but they're worth looking at."

A cry rang out from the back bedroom.

"Well, sounds like Pauly's awake; it's feeding time. Will you check on Keith? He has been quiet in your room…too quiet."

Maureen smiled and went around the corner, and quickly returned. "He is asleep on the floor, lying on his blanket."

"That's a relief. He needed a nap. He woke up too early. Sometimes I wish you all could just wake up at the same time, like around eight in the morning would be nice."

Shaking her head, Maureen added, "You know that won't ever happen with all of these boys around. No problem for us girls."

Virginia frowned. "I suppose."

Chapter 4

Burns and Stitches

Now settled in for a few years, around 1969, the news was mixed with excitement and turmoil. Apollo 9 through 11 successfully landed on the moon and returned home to a ticker tape parade. Sirhan Sirhan was convicted of killing Robert Kennedy, and Yasser Arafat was appointed Palestine Liberation Organized leader. Lastly, the US Air Force program, Project Blue Book, closed its study of UFOs.

During these crazy times, the youngest children were now walking and talking. Peace and quiet were desired commodities. The only quiet time came in the late hours when everyone was in bed. No human would want Virginia's inconsistent sleeping arrangements and durations with their shared bedroom living.

In the tiny Yucaipa house, Virginia shared the one queen bed with Cynthia or alternated to the living room couch. Whenever she found the moment to doze, she took advantage. Good and uninterrupted sleep was rare; she often dreamt about it while awake.

With cereal being a go-to breakfast for the kids, her oldest children were responsible for pouring milk for the younger ones. Virginia again strained every morsel of sleep a few times, but it seldom worked.

One sure reason was the trustworthy cock-a-doodle-doo of the local roosters. Virginia often wondered if those pesky creatures knew when the crack of dawn was. This was a Yucaipa norm. She preferred the cooing of the mourning doves. Their songs were much more pleasant and almost soothed her back to sleep. But on cue, the rude feathered rooster screeched at the strangest hours.

The nights for Virginia, especially the late-night, when all was quiet, was when dark worries crept in. Lying still and staring at the ceiling, Cynthia's go-to method of trying to fall asleep, kept her awake. Her daughter repeatedly banged her head on the pillow. Although it worked for her, Virginia, many nights, would gently hold her hand on Cynthia's head, kindly letting her know enough was enough.

She tossed and chased the comfort of sleep. But Virginia's insides ached with worry, and nerves often strangled her. Some nights, when the worries were so terrible, her insides felt like they boiled over. So, she would quietly climb out of bed, sneak to the restroom, and vomit.

Maureen and Cynthia would hear her cry as well. Fearful of bothering her, they understood she needed time to herself and some things they couldn't fix. They didn't understand grown-up matters. They seemed foreign and made no sense to them. They did all they could to help, even trying to make their mom smile, but her magnitude of hurt was out of their reach. It still upset them, making it hard to see her this way. It even took its toll on the girls. Maureen wondered if the boys even knew.

One night, after a late-night episode, Virginia climbed back in bed over Cynthia, who was awake. Cynthia, of all her children, heard mom the most. She finally gained courage and quietly asked, "Mommy, are you okay?"

A heavy sigh passed, and Virginia whispered, "Yes, I'm all right, dear. Sometimes I..." She paused. "You go to sleep, Cynthia. Don't you worry. It'll be okay."

"I love you, Mommy," Cynthia whispered back.

"I love you too. See you in the morning."

Rolling over and dreading to know the time, Virginia squeezed her eyes shut and forced sleep to come.

~

Virginia opened her eyes, and an unusual quiet ruled the air. She looked around the bedroom, and the girls were already up. She listened intently and could barely hear faint whispers. *Is that bacon I smell?*

Curious, she rubbed her tired eyes, and acid began up her throat. Slowly, she climbed out of bed and headed for the heartburn medicine. She noticed the kids were already up, being quiet as mice. The little T.V. was on, and four children huddled in close, trying to listen to cartoons. Cynthia sat at the table drawing.

Virginia stumbled to the restroom, downed some medicine, and proceeded through the crowd.

The kids all smiled and whispered, *Good morning.*

"What is this? You're all unusually quiet this early." She returned the smile.

Paul jumped up and hugged one leg and Keith the other. "We already had breakfast, too," Keith said.

Maureen approached. "We know you aren't feeling well. We wanted to help. Please, Mom, we want you to get some rest."

Virginia dropped her head and wore a half-smile. "You kids are so wonderful...thank you. The problem is, I can't sleep anymore. I'll have some breakfast and enjoy the peace and quiet. Is that bacon I smell?"

"I think I will make some oatmeal to settle my stomach," Virginia said as she pulled the oatmeal box out and added water to the small pot.

She looked out the window, and it was a beautiful morning. She slid open the kitchen window, and they could hear the familiar dove coo.

After she set the pot on the stove, she turned on the electric burner. She opened the fridge and stared. *Maybe I should just have a little milk. I shouldn't have coffee, yuck, too acidy,* she thought.

Maureen turned the burner off, put the bacon on a plate, and set it on the table. Virginia smiled at the kind gesture.

Placing slices of bread in the toaster, she looked again at her quiet kids. Smiling and almost uncomfortable with the quiet, she mused, *I can get used to this, but, like always, it's too good to be true.*

She opened the oatmeal container, measured the portion, and turned to the pot. The toaster popped, and she jumped. *Goodness,* she thought as she spun back and whacked the handle of the bacon frying pan, causing hot oil to fly in every direction.

Stinging, burning grease splashed up her right arm. Instant pain shot to her brain as she screamed. The pan fell to the floor, the remaining oil splattered on her pajama leg, and she ran for the sink.

Maureen jumped from the table.

Patrick rushed in and saw the danger. "Stay back!" he yelled to the younger and turned and picked up the pan.

"Get me some ice!" Virginia cried.

Maureen's heart ached as she went for the drawer and grabbed a clean washcloth while Patrick seized the ice. He rushed it to her as she finished running cold water on the wound…she cringed at the damage. She was severely burned, from her elbow down, on the front to the delicate part of the skin. The bulk of the grease was a dead aim on her tender arm. Tears welled in Maureen's eyes as mom sat at the dining room table.

"Oh, Maureen, don't worry." Virginia wrapped the ice and slowly caressed the damage. She gritted her teeth in great pain but remained quiet.

"Greg, grab the mop, and let's get the floor clean," Patrick ordered as the other kids stood to the side and didn't know what to do.

They had never seen Mom hurt. They were always the ones with booboos, and it seemed scary seeing her in pain. All they wanted to do was hug her. It was new, and they didn't like the look of it. It was out of their league, and they felt helpless.

The kids funneled to the outdoors once the danger settled, and the day pressed on.

Virginia nursed her already stressful stomach illness and now a burned arm. She sat at the table and stared out the window. *Can things get any worse?*

I wouldn't ask if I were you. They can get a lot worse, Virginia.

"Mom," Maureen startled her.

"Oh! You made me jump."

"Sorry, but have you eaten?"

Virginia shrugged. "I guess I haven't."

"Well, it's lunchtime. I'll make you a sandwich with lots of mustard. The way you like it," she said as she turned and went to the kitchen.

The night pressed on with agony. Virginia tried to make herself comfortable to sleep, so she reclined in a chair that night. But the pain kept her awake. Before she knew it, the idiot rooster's clock was way off again. Her eyelids stretched open at 3 a.m. "Good grief!" she grumbled as she slowly adjusted her pillow. "Please, I need to sleep."

Silence suddenly ruled as she opened her eyes. The sun was up, and to her surprise, she slept. The pain quickly reminded her of the accident the day before, and she moaned. Slowly, she pulled herself up and opened the curtain. *No going to church this morning*, she thought as the sun slowly began to beam.

She checked on her children. They were sacked from the long and emotional day before. Pain leaped to her head as she accidentally brushed her wound across her pajamas.

"Ouch." Not wanting to wake her kids, she bit her lip and suppressed her outburst.

She slowly looked closely at her arm. "This can't be good."

The coffee percolator bubbled while she went outside into the cold air to fetch the Sunday paper. Wooziness draped around her head. She paused before she picked up the paper and took a deep breath. *God, what did I do to deserve this? I know it's not Your fault, but I can't ever seem to catch a break. I am sorry for complaining. What do I do?*

While morning larks sang aloud, she gazed at the San Gorgonio mountains and said, "I wish I could just be well."

Thump!

"Ouch!" She stubbed her toe on the pavement and almost fell to the ground. "How on earth do I do this to myself?"

Another pain was realized as her unbandaged arm smudged across the front of the newspaper. "Yuck."

Staring close at her wound, the wiggly and dangling skin and running ooze made her stomach turn. *I can't go to the hospital, I never paid for Pauly, and they probably all know this. Darn it, Virginia, why did you ever walk out?*

Sickness began to boil the acids in her stomach as she headed back to the front door when she heard Betty, her neighbor, call her name.

"Hey Virginia, you're up early this morning." She walked over, holding a basket.

"Good morning, yes, I am, but at least you're dressed. Forgive me. I look like a wreck." Virginia used her free hand to try and fix her hair.

"You look fine. Anyway, I was gathering eggs and wanted to give you a dozen. I was going to sneak them on your porch, but I heard you yelp. You all right?" A long pause followed as Virginia hid her arm.

"Okay, Virginia. What did you do?"

Looking at Betty and then up to the mountains, she fought her stubbornness. Virginia paused, wondering if she should tell her.

Betty frowned. "Okay, fine, you can keep your secrets. Here are your eggs!" she said, handing the basket over.

Reaching for the basket while also holding the newspaper Virginia cringed. "Well, I have one good arm. Could you set them inside for me?"

"All right, Virginia, stop being stubborn and tell me where you are hurt."

Slowly, she revealed the burn, and Betty let out a cry. "Goodness gracious, what on earth…how did you burn yourself? That looks horrible. Did you see a doctor yet?"

Embarrassed, Virginia nervously looked into her front window to make sure curious eyes weren't spying on her. "I, um, I never told you that I snuck out of the hospital when I gave birth to Pauly. Meaning…I never paid for my delivery. The social worker wanted to give my children away… so, I can't go back, ever, to a hospital…they'll find out?" Panicked that she finally told someone who was not family, she looked down in shame.

Betty's heart sank. "Virginia, that was what, four or five years ago? In a different city? Your arm looks infected. You have to go, and I'm going to take you…now!"

"No, I'm not going to the hospital," Virginia protested.

"Stubborn woman! I'm at least taking you to the clinic in town, and don't argue! You will be dead if that arm isn't treated or an amputee. How would you take care of six kids with one arm?"

"Darn it. You're right. I wouldn't survive with one arm. I'm barely surviving now!" Feeling flustered and still embarrassed, she said, "I'll change and wake Maureen. This Sunday morning has turned out to be a…"

She caught herself in her misery and realized that Betty was doing a kind thing. Turning to face Betty, she said, "Really, I'm thankful for your help. I suppose you're my answer to my prayer, and sorry for being such a crab."

"Heck, Virginia, if I were in your shoes trying to raise six munchkins, I'd be dead by now. Raising my four boys has nearly killed me already! Not to mention wanting to strangle them every day. I, of course, don't want to go to prison for murder," she joked. "Those are my worries. Let's quit squawking and get a move on. Come over when you are ready. I'll be in the car."

The drive to the clinic was brief, and Virginia's nerves were rearing up. The unsettling always started in her guts and then moved to her head.

As they pulled into the driveway, she began to feel nauseous. That was more from the great hospital escape rather than her injury. She braced herself for the uncertain journey through the door.

The nurse called Virginia in. Suspicious of the doctor, she waited for him to mention that he knew she was a hospital escapee. But as the minutes passed by, he never said a word.

Much to her relief, the visit was brief. The kind doctor concurred that her arm was terrible, as suspected, and was glad she came in when she did. They painfully cleaned and correctly dressed her wound, and the medicine helped. He instructed her to return in a few days for a checkup, and she obliged.

After leaving the clinic, she kept a nervous eye over her shoulder. She couldn't let go of her hospital escape doubts. Feelings like this were complicated for her to shake, she would have never dreamed of not paying a hospital bill, but the guilt remained.

Great rejoicing abounded when she returned, and the bunch wanted to know what the clinic was like. Question after question rang out until it became overwhelming.

Maureen stepped in and said, "Give mom some rest. We will answer your questions later."

Virginia felt relief and thankfulness. She went into the bedroom and shut the door. Lying on the bed, she took one deep breath, closed her eyes, and was out.

Deep sleep took her away, and when her eyes finally opened, she thought, *I haven't moved an inch. Is it evening time?*

She quickly stood. "I can't believe I actually slept that long," she muttered.

A sudden rush of panic overwhelmed her. "My kids!"

She rushed and opened the door, and a scent caught her attention. *Is that dinner I smell?*

As she stepped out, she saw her kids were, once again, quietly watching TV. The panic left her as her heart slowed, and she was beyond impressed.

Maureen said, "Hello," while preparing the evening meal, which was much appreciated. "Mom, for the sake of your health, please stay out of the kitchen tonight. I have it handled."

Virginia chuckled and agreed.

Despite all she had gone through, she looked at each of her children's faces and realized they were genuinely incredible. *How blessed am I to have all six of these children?* she thought. *I would do anything for them.*

They were learning and retaining what she taught them.

Her heart beamed with joy as they helped with the dish settings, cooking, laughter, and saying grace before the meal. She truly loved her children, despite the hardships and peril that lurked around every corner of every morning. These brief moments of peace were treasured.

A few weeks passed, and the burn was reduced to a deep redness. Virginia's spirits were lifted again, and there was a great delight in feeling better.

But, with six children, horseplay was growing rampant in the home. As long as nobody was hurt, Virginia was at ease. With her mother's ear always attuned to their play, she could decipher when someone was being teased and crying, joking, real or fake laughter, and the dreaded hurt cry.

The kids were extra rowdy this Saturday morning. Yelling at them ensued to take it out into the yard. Her endless chore list was being checked off one by one as she nervously listened to the outside for any faint scream or unwanted cry. But, to her relief, none came, and soon the sun set.

It was time for the Saturday evening baths, and the kids came inside. With only one tub, every cleansing was done in shifts. The oldest first, then the youngest, always went last and shared the tub time. It saved water and time. Virginia knew the water would be a gross tinge of brown. She drained it and would fill it for the next, and so on.

The kids managed to tame their crazy excitement for a while, but someone suggested a game of tag. Virginia's familiar voice rang out, "NO RUNNING IN THE HOUSE!"

Trying to speed walk while the others were escaping, the tagger, Paul, the youngest, couldn't keep up since he was so little.

Virginia finished getting ready for bed, then moved into the kitchen to begin putting dishes away. The laughter halted by a sudden *thud*! Next, a blood-curdling scream cut loose.

"Pauly!" Virginia's heart stopped as she ran to the bathroom.

He stood there with blood covering his face and dripping onto his shirt. His hands were also covered as the expression of shock consumed his little bloody face. Tears began pouring out like a waterfall.

"What happened?" Virginia asked, trying to contain the panic in her voice.

Keith stood fiddling with his hands in nervousness as his eyes paced back and forth, trying to explain. "Well, while chasing me, I guess he tripped over his coat lying on the floor. His head hit the corner of the bedpost."

Quickly, with her heart racing, she grabbed the washrag and searched for the source of the torrent of blood. Washing Paul's face and calming him down, she found the cut was over his right eye. Unfortunately, it was a large gash that she knew no bandage would cure.

She dialed her neighbor, got dressed, and her heart sank. "Maureen, you're in charge, and the rest of you, to bed!"

"Mom, can I come and help?" Greg asked.

Pausing, she said, "Yes, thank you. Get dressed and hurry!"

Virginia could use all the help she could get, so having Greg come would help the situation.

Speeding to the same clinic, she rushed him in. After examining the wound, the doctor announced that it would be around twelve stitches. Laying cloth over Paul's face and exposing the wound, he broke out a needle and was approaching to numb his skin. Greg's eyes bugged at the sight of it.

The doctor began to administer the needle. Greg immediately asked about the syringe, and Virginia quickly raised her index finger to her lips to hush him. There was no way more grief would come to her already traumatized son.

Greg nodded and understood.

Virginia stared, wondering if there would be a day when this pace would ever slow down. *Oh, maybe when they are grown and gone, I will have peace and quiet, or I'll be dead first.*

"Virginia, be careful what you wish for," she whispered.

The doctor finished, and Paul whimpered.

Greg looked closely at the stitches. "Far out! I dig your stitches!"

"Gregory, don't bring attention to it!" she scolded. Looking at Paul, she already knew where this was heading. His countenance changed from, *woe is me,* to that, *Hey, this will get me special attention.*

Virginia shook her head.

Stepping into the front door at home, Virginia knew no one would be sleeping. True to form, the troops were lined up to see Paul's stitches, and he was eating up every bit of the attention.

Patrick eagerly asked, "Did it hurt when they stuck the needle in your skin?"

Paul looked dumbfounded, not realizing what had taken place at the clinic. "Mommy, did they stitch my skin?" he wondered.

"Pauly, that's what stitches are. You know, needle and thread."

Looking far off, everyone now was laughing at his young ignorance. He quickly went from a hero to a goof. But he couldn't help but laugh, and finally, they scurried off to bed.

It was now late, and they had to attend church the next day.

"Pauly?" Virginia calmly called him over.

Yawning, he slowly walked to her. Gently she set him on her lap and cradled him closely. She didn't speak but held him tightly as if sheltering him from all the pain in the world.

Sleepily, he snuggled in close to her. His aching stitches seemed forgotten as he drifted to sleep, safe in his mother's arms.

Chapter 5

Foxhole and Battle Plans

The weekends, to the six children, were viewed as a rite of passage to the next creative quest. With this bunch, what to play seemed to stir profoundly by Thursday nights. They plotted and schemed to pick one of the many offered ideas. No time was wasted unless chores, restrictions, or punishment somehow interfered with playing.

On one of those weekends, on Friday after school, the final concept was accepted by the brotherhood of Patrick and Greg, and the only thing they needed was the morning to come. The younger siblings always approved of the ideas because they knew that whatever big brothers concocted would be fun if they were allowed to join.

Certain Friday nights were filled with Virginia's wonderful treat of homemade popcorn and The Wonderful World of Disney when afforded. Sure, they watched other shows, like Adam-12, Bonanza, or an occasional Green Acres, which usually the kids didn't understand. But old Disney spoke kid language.

By Virginia's guidance, the kids would pull the wagon to Food-Fair, and she would let each child pick one can of Shasta soda. The choices then seemed endless. There was cola, orange, root beer, lemon-lime, crème soda, red raspberry, and black cherry. When pressed for time, this was not an easy task, but the choices became more manageable, and they all wanted to be different.

The high anticipation for the sun to set and the programs to start seemed forever. Since sodas were not a standard beverage, it was only water, iced tea, and powdered milk. Sipping from the sweet nectar of flavored carbonated drink was an expensive delicacy in the household.

The youngest would sip slowly to savor the sugary liquid and stretch it as long as possible. But, like always, it seemed to disappear quickly. Then, back to water.

One time, Paul spilled his favored orange drink and whaled and groaned. Virginia reminded everyone to use two hands. Paul, being little and both hands slippery with butter, most of the time never listened and paid for it dearly. His long face drooped to the floor, watching everyone else slurping their soda, and Virginia would yell, "Stop pouting!"

Saturday mornings were like a tidal wave for playing and stretching every ounce of sunlight to build or create. Every Saturday morning began a new chapter to be written. This particular weekend the outside screamed to come and play.

Patrick and Greg hatched their great idea of building something entirely new for them. This build had to allow them to hide from the enemy and have room for a 50-caliber machine gun to mow down the adversary as if they were in a shooting gallery.

This exquisite plan was a covert operation that needed the highest clearance before they would share it. One enormous obstacle faced them, their mother. In their minds, they began sketching out the foxhole's size, depths, and dimensions. This foxhole would be the grandest, deepest, and safest ever constructed to save them from the onslaught of the much-hated enemy who opposed their military tactics.

They needed to dig right away. The hardest challenge was where to build it so they could save the world from their foe. If they dug anywhere in their yard, they would surely be caught since the last time they dug an army tunnel, Virginia had a conniption.

That story of the famed army escape tunnel happened sometime earlier in the year, on the east side of the front yard. The older boys began to dig a giant hole. Once they were down several feet, the tunnel construction began to head north. This new escape tunnel would for sure free the prisoners. There would be no need for Steve Macqueen to jump his motorcycle over the barbwire fence to flee the enemy, like in The Great Escape. This tunnel would provide a clean and comfortable porthole to freedom.

As the engineered beauty commenced, dirt flew and began darkening the yard, which confirmed significant progress. Next, they barked orders to the young cadets, Keith, and Paul, to get them this or bring over that, and the two fulfilled their duties.

Cynthia soon joined the fray, and her enlistment was an added value. Greg entrusted her with the ever-important mission of obtaining inner liners for the tunnel. "Can you handle this command, soldier?" Greg asked.

"Sir, yes, sir!" Cynthia saluted and disappeared in secrecy.

As the dirt kept flying and the tunnel grew longer, Cynthia returned with a few bedsheets that Greg and Patrick utilized for the floor and ceiling after they dug the second opening. Now complete, the tunnel was used to transport the prisoners to freedom.

"Cynthia, Keith, and Paul line up for escape!" Patrick directed them.

Greg was their guide. Jumping into the hole, one by one, the cold earth welcomed them as they entered. Ducking and crawling on the pegged-in sheets made the whole experience luxurious. No dirt falling from the ceiling and their clothes not getting filthy seemed a bit of a rip-off, but the thrill was higher than ever as they began popping out on the other side. After the escape, they ran around the house and pretended to be captured again until shouts from the enemy came from the front door.

"Oh no, we have been caught…for real!" Greg shouted as the enemy, Virginia, quickly arrived in a frantic charge.

"What have you done?!" she yelled, bending down and peering into the gaping hole. "Boys! You get this hole filled immediately! It could collapse, and you could suffocate!"

With her hands on her hips, she was serious, and all the hard labor and escape plans were foiled.

Virginia sped away into the house. Slowly, what seemed easy digging for hours to construct the tunnel, now seemed like hard labor. Shackled in verbal irons, the backfilling had begun, and the entire entrance was packed in. Next, they mournfully began on the escape hole.

Gone was the thrill and excitement, and the work continued until Greg shouted, "Wait!" He jumped into the last hole before it was filled in and a spark of hope arose. "Bury me up to my head!"

Laughter erupted, and it suddenly did not seem like work, and sure enough, before they knew it, the only part of Greg that showed was his neck and head, and the kids laughed hard.

Mom was summoned one last time, and she quickly came.

Stopping in her tracks, she said, "What? What is it? I see you filled up the hole?"

The kids, blocking Greg's buried body, giggled as they slowly moved sideways; there, to her horror, was Greg. "Gregory, David! You unbury him now!"

But this time, a sudden smile appeared, and she shook her head. She couldn't help but laugh at the sight of Greg's head sticking out of the ground like a plant. The other children's laughter was quite contagious too.

She turned and stopped again, this time in great anger. "Good gracious, are these my bed sheets? They're ruined!"

So, with that back story now explained, you see why the new construction of the foxhole needed to employ a different strategy, and it was soon hatched. This strategy required incorporating the neighbor boy, Johnny, and his yard. His yard was massive, with old barns and a horse corral, the same one that held Cindy, the snapping pony they all feared.

Johnny's easy recruitment meant that the building would start immediately. With excavation tools in hand and marching through the opening in the hedges, Greg pinpointed the spot. After surveying how the enemy could be defeated, the groundbreaking began.

"How deep do we go?" Greg asked.

"At least two feet deep and six feet wide. We need lots of room while firing on the enemy. We can't be bumping into each other." Patrick surveyed and then began digging.

A collective "Yeah" was heard as they moved large amounts of dirt.

Patrick barked orders as his comrades dug harder. "We need that wall straighter, and our hole is looking like an egg. The dirt here is too high; it needs to be spread out."

The soil was flying out of the hole in three different ways. Soon, a collective stop was ordered. "I'm thirsty." Patrick leaped out of the hole and headed for the hose.

Greg hit a large rock with his shovel. It kept him from going deeper. "Let me move this rock. Then I will get a drink."

Johnny tried to work the edges with his hoe.

Greg and Johnny bumped.

"Hey, watch it, chump, you're in my way!" Johnny pushed.

"I'm trying to get this dumb rock out, sorry." Greg moved over, bent, and began to dig with his fingers. Clearing the edges of the rock and feeling he could get a grip to unearth it, he pulled and pulled.

Again, Johnny yelled, "Get out of my space! You're in my way!"

Oblivious to his rant, Greg was feeling victory over the rock, and with one last tug, out of the corner of his eye, Johnny had his hoe raised above his head and yelled, "I said, get out of my way!"

A sudden sting and blunt force knocked Greg over as Johnny's hoe clobbered him in the head. With stinging pain, blood oozed from the top of Greg's skull. Feeling woozy, Greg was in shock that the enemy was in his foxhole.

Patrick quickly ran back from the house. "What the heck are you doing!"

He jumped in and shoved Johnny to the ground. He quickly helped Greg out of the hole. Scanning his head, he grimaced over the deep cut, and large amounts of blood poured from the wound.

Standing in a dazed fog, Johnny had the look of, *I don't know why I did that.* The boyish rules of personal space and the feeling that no one listens drove him to his dastardly deed. He was speechless.

Patrick burst through the door, screaming, "Mom! Greg is bleeding!"

Virginia dropped the pans and sped into the room. The siblings surrounded Greg as his tears subsided, and Virginia looked mortified. "Quickly now, into the bathroom."

She grabbed a washcloth and the much-hated peroxide and doused the cut with the antiseptic, which burned like fire. In her comforting way, she knew when to blow on it to bring cooling, to spare her children from the peak antiseptic burn.

Betty, Johnny's mother, knocked on the door. "Is Greg okay? I'm so sorry. Johnny said it was an accident."

Virginia defended her child, "Not likely, Betty, Greg said he did it on purpose, and Patrick watched him do it! We can discuss it later, but for now, I need to take him to the clinic, and I can't afford it. Maybe you can drive us, or I'll have to call my sister."

Betty obliged, and they were on another joyous cruise to the clinic.

The bleeding was slowing, but Virginia knew it needed stitches. *This is all I need, more bills to pay with the money I don't have.*

Greg seemed to calm down but was in charge of holding the washcloth on his bleeding scalp.

Pulling into the local clinic, they hurried him inside and looked at the damage.

The doctor said, "Hello, Virginia. This is becoming a bit frequent."

"Trust me. This is the last place on earth I want to be," Virginia snapped.

The doctor smirked. "I know. Okay, let's have a look. Yes, it will need stitches. We will numb him, so he won't feel a thing. Maybe a little tugging here and there, but that's all."

Greg lay on the same table as his little brother had several months earlier, and the doctor went to work.

Virginia stared as she feared these days would keep happening. Knowing she couldn't prevent accidents that may befall her kids since there were so many. So far, it had been burns, bumps, bruises, and stitches, but no broken bones…yet.

The doctor shaved the back of Greg's head and completed the stitches. He helped Greg up and told him he would be fine.

At least it's a short trip this time and in the afternoon. And not the middle of the night, Virginia thought.

They drove home, and all the others wanted to ogle at the damaged area of Greg's skull.

After many remarks about how cool it looked, Greg wore the wound proudly. "It didn't hurt that bad," he bravely stated. "You know, I might have to kick Johnny's butt for this!"

Virginia belted out, "Gregory, there will be no such thing. You stay away from that brat if he's going to treat you like this!"

She stormed away to start dinner, but to her surprise, Maureen and Cynthia had already begun and were on their way to completion.

Virginia stopped and paused with great delight. There was always so much to do, and unpredictable interferences were happening far more often than Virginia would like. Many mouths still needed to be fed, and the girls knew when to step in and help. Moments like these brought joy to Virginia's heart. She often wondered if she was raising all her children right, and with selfless actions like Maureen and Cynthia's at this moment, she knew she was.

With another tragedy now over, Virginia helped the girls finish cooking. She never wanted her children to be hungry. Always cooking and planning the meals for the troops was front and foremost in her mind.

She slowed to a stop and looked at Maureen and Cynthia. "Thank you. Really, thanks so much for your help. Without it, I would lose my mind."

They set the dishes on the two dining room tables. Yes, two. When Frankie moved out, she left one of them, so Virginia combined the two to seat seven in the small dining room. They were placed like a T. After calling on the others to help.

Special treatment was given to Greg. Some were jealous, and some wished they were the ones hurt so they could get special treatment. When so many were competing for attention, it seemed a great idea to be wounded in some way. Not life-threatening, of course, but even those thoughts ran through their minds.

That week, Virginia and Betty would not allow their boys to play, but the following Saturday, the finishing work of the bloodstained foxhole would commence.

Patrick stepped through the hedgerow and called for Johnny, and he sped around the corner, excited to finish the dig. Patrick looked stern. "Why did you hit my brother?"

"It was an accident, I swear!"

On and on Johnny went, trying to plead his case, but since that incident, suspicions reigned. Both brothers knew never again to turn their backs on him.

With work almost finished, they dug to the needed depths. Greg's head throbbed, but that wouldn't stop him from accomplishing the mission. They reached their goal with a cautious eye on Johnny and sweat on Greg's brow.

"We need to cover it like a fort!" Johnny sped away and returned with a pinkish blanket.

"That's all you can find? That sucks?" Patrick protested. "That looks too babyish!"

"Beggars can't be choosers," Johnny retorted.

The battle began with flinging the very non-military covering over the hole.

As they imagined the enemy approaching when the war finally started, Johnny's mom and dad had to leave for a while, and the boys knew that playtime would be much longer. Excitement peaked as they began loading their imaginary machine guns, and the foxhole lived up to the hype.

Noisy rockets and explosions reigned down as a strange enemy suddenly attacked. Johnny's large Great Dane, Brutus, came barking profusely out of his cage. Snapping his T-rex jaw under the blanket, the boys shrank away from the menace.

Johnny yelled at him, "Stop it, dumb dog! Get out-a-here, Brutus!"

Brutus circled the hole and barked like a rabid dog. The boys were trapped, and Johnny's commands were useless. He was a gargantuan monster who brought fear to most but only sometimes was cool to the boys. This particular day, however, anger stirred him as his barking demanded that no one leave the hole.

A few minutes passed and then an hour.

"What do we do, Johnny? He's your idiot dog!" Greg yelled.

"He's not an idiot, you jerk!" Johnny fumed.

"Oh yeah, then step out of the hole and see what your idiot dog will do? Well, go ahead...you big fat chicken!" Greg dared.

"All right, I will."

Johnny swallowed hard and commanded Brutus to sit, stay, or whatever other commands he could think of. Looking back at Patrick and Greg, Johnny said, "Here I go, watch how he minds me."

He lifted the blanket and stared straight up. Brutus leaped at him. Johnny kept commanding while taking his first step out, but Brutus fastened his giant jaw around his head and clamped down.

Johnny screamed in pain and fell back into the hole, covered in slobber. Quickly folding the flap back over, he backpedaled to the boys.

"Yep, he's an idiot," Greg assured, and Johnny didn't argue. "Well, now, what do we do?"

"You're not bleeding, Johnny," Patrick affirmed. "Maybe you should whack him in the head with the hoe."

The boys laughed, and Johnny sulked.

Patrick's great mind hatched another strategic plan. "Let's make a dash for the shed! We should all go at the same time."

After much protest, they agreed. It was the only plan they had.

First-order was to remain reticent. They listened hard, and they found all was deathly silent. In a whisper, they counted down to three, two, one. Pulling the blanket back and ready to jump out of the hole, Brutus was already standing in their way.

"Ah!" the boys yelled and quickly fell back into the hole and covered up.

Greg chimed in, "I gotta pee, and I'm starved!"

Hours went by, and nothing seemed to work. Was this the battle that they wouldn't have victory over? Truly they were at war.

"I know what to do!" Johnny began to yell, "Help! Help us!"

Patrick and Greg looked at each other, shook their heads, and sighed.

Another long spell passed, and no one came. Finally, after hearing his parents driving up, all three boys began to scream for their dear lives. As loud as they possibly could, the call for surrender echoed through Yucaipa until Johnny's dad approached and pulled Brutus away.

"How long have you been stuck in that hole?" he inquired.

"Ever since you left." Johnny crawled out.

Looking dumbfounded, his dad remarked, "You're kidding. That was hours ago."

Patrick and Greg jumped out and took off running. They sprinted home to the single bathroom and kitchen for food.

And so, the war ended, and the foxhole was deemed too dangerous, as long as Brutus was free.

Soon after, the neighbors built a pool in that very place, putting an end to the endless battles and sieges of the enemy, and sealing it for good.

Chapter 6

The Bad Men

In 1971, gas was 40 cents a gallon, and peanut butter was 60 cents. A brand-new Dodge Charger was $2500.00. A massive earthquake hit the San Fernando Valley shaking Southern California, and killed over fifty people. Virginia's nerves were always on edge.

This year, her baby, Paul, turned five and could enter kindergarten. Going to school and being able to finally ride the bus made him feel grown-up, like his brothers and sisters. He liked to pretend he was older and braver, but when his siblings teased him, and he felt outnumbered, his greatest defense was hiding behind Virginia for safety.

The start of the school year was new and exciting for Paul. He received his first lunch pail and guaranteed — it was never brand new, always a hand-me-down. Being the youngest, just about everything he was given had been broken-in, three times over. Duct tape did wonders for old sneakers and inner liners on jackets.

Virginia frowned as she fussed with his hair and wet the cowlick above his forehead. "Well, this thing won't cooperate. Why does it have to be on the front of your head? I swear, it has a mind of its own. You will just have to live with it. Get your lunch pail, and I will walk you to the bus stop."

"I wish I could walk myself," he mumbled.

"Pauly! When you have done it several times, then I will let you like the older kids. But for now, you are stuck with me."

They headed down the long drive with Keith and Cynthia and west on Ave. E. They stayed on the right side of the road, close to the gutter. There were about five houses along the way until they reached the parking lot of the small church.

Virginia stopped, firmly squeezed his hand, and said, "Okay, your bus stop is across the street. You, first. Look both ways, and when there are no cars, then you can cross."

Looking up and down Ave E, Paul didn't see a car in sight. In those days, roads were not busy. Paul thought, *I don't ever see any cars.*

Stepping across the street, they stood under a fruit tree and waited. Soon, another mother arrived, and then a few more kids who seemed to be older. All had their hair brushed and were clean, ready for the first day of school.

Hopping on the bus was beyond exciting for Paul. This was something he couldn't wait to do. Oblivious to his brother and sister, he chose his seat and stared hard out the window with sheer fascination. Being able to drive places was a rarity, and this adventure was rated as number one in his mind.

Sitting high on the bus and looking down at cars was almost like flying. Soon, his imagination ruled, and Paul was suddenly clothed in a cape. Ascending and descending over houses and down gullies and for some strange reason, quickly, his fantasy came to a screeching halt. *What happened? Why did we stop?*

An ocean of students buzzed about while pouring from the row of buses. To his amazement, they were already at Valley Elementary school. *That was fast.*

Cynthia said, "Paul, follow me, and I will show you the ropes."

"What are the ropes for?" Paul looked around.

"No silly, not real ropes. I will show you what to do. That's what it means." Cynthia laughed.

She guided him off the bus and to his class. With an eagerness for the next adventure, the smiling teacher welcomed him to the playful pupils.

Quickly, he took to his classmates and loved story time. Listening to the teacher's every word was easy at first, but slowly he tired, and his imagination took over. His eyes caught the play center, complete with wooden cabinets odd to him; they were miniature, fitting his size. Not knowing something like this existed, he immediately captured a dream that this was his house, he had a wife, and all of the students were their kids. The next thing he knew, the kids were standing, and he was dumbfounded. *What happened to the story? Is it over?* he thought.

Clueless to the school ways, laughter rang as the kids ran outside. Paul couldn't figure out what the students were doing. Looking for the teacher's permission, she smiled and said, "Paul, it's recess time. You may go use the restroom or go outside on the playground."

He turned to leave. *Playground?*

Paul stepped into the patio. Over to the right was a colossal steel monkey bars set. With wide eyes and a happy smile, he ran to the mountain of kids and climbed to its highest point. Looking out over the sea of onlookers, he ruled the top.

Suddenly, watching the descending kids, he asked, *Where are they going?*

Playtime had ended, and the herds were returning to class. Planting an imaginary flag to claim the top, Paul left his flag blowing in the wind and vowed to return and claim his territory soon.

School ended in the afternoon, and he stepped off the bus. Virginia met him at his stop with a smile. He ran into his mother's arms and couldn't speak fast enough of the great things that had happened. Marvelous stories of fascinating bus rides and pretending to live with a vast family with his mini kitchen play-center poured forth—lastly, the monkey bars.

Virginia and Paul stepped into the house. She asked, "That's very exciting. Now, what did you learn? Was there writing and math? Did the teacher read a story to you? If so, what was it about."

A long pause hovered at these strange words. *What did I learn? Hmm…*

Virginia shook her head because she knew he was a daydreamer. "Pauly, you're going to school to learn, not just play. You have weekends to play now. You're a student. I want you to listen to your teacher and pay attention to your lessons. It's not hours of daydreaming and playing. You're in kindergarten to begin learning. Is that understood?"

"Yes, Momma," he said with his head bowed.

He began the long march to the kitchen to clean his lunch pail. As he emptied the contents, he pretended they were treasured spoils of the new land he claimed on the monkey bars…he grinned.

When Cynthia and Keith returned home, Paul shared what he liked about school. Keith added he also enjoyed the old playground in kindergarten. But, to Paul's delight, Keith informed him that when he gets to first grade, there's a much larger set of monkey bars far out on the vast lawn. Paul gasped with excitement and suddenly wanted to skip a grade.

Paul was in full swing of school life, and the art of pretending to learn was plotting along nicely. Virginia let him walk with his brother and sister to the bus stop, and she also began, on occasion, to let him walk home with the other students since their class let out in the afternoon.

One day during story time, important law enforcement officers donning gold badges stood next to the teacher as they explained some dark stories.

A sheriff began, "My name is Sheriff Mike, and this is my partner, Sheriff Dave. You children, listen closely. You have all heard of bad guys. They're real, and we have a sad local story to tell you. There are men, evil men, who try to steal children by tricking them with candy. Please hear me, don't let them fool you. If you fall for their tricks, they may try and steal you and do bad things."

As he kept speaking, Paul's daydreaming caused him to imagine a bad guy attacking. He would slug him in the nose, then another punch to his jaw. Then he laughed at the sight of the bad guy doubling over in pain of death. Finally, he envisioned himself wearing the important uniform, shoving the bad guys behind prison bars.

The Sheriff finished his story with, "So, are we clear? That story is unfortunate, so please don't end up like this little girl. Thank you, be safe." The Sheriffs smiled and exited.

Little girl? What happened to the little girl?

Paul, you need to pay attention and learn, he heard his mother's voice.

He raised his hand and asked, "Teacher, can you tell the story of the little girl again?"

Many others agreed, and she sighed. "The little girl was walking alone, and the bad men pulled alongside her and offered her candy. She, being naive, walked to their car and took the candy, when suddenly they sprang from their car and kidnapped her. She was never found."

A collective gasp arose as fear and horror ran over their small minds. What a scary thing to happen, and sadness ruled Paul's heart. *Maybe I should not have asked. This is sad. If I could, I would rescue the little girl.*

He imagined the girl with blonde hair, a fluffy white dress, and white shoes. His heart sank, and all he could think of was this story.

The day flew by, and later that night, he told his mom. Sadly, Virginia confirmed the story was true. "Never ever take anything from strangers. Most people are nice and would help you with any need. But there are also bad people, and they only mean to harm you."

"But will she be found?" His round eyes were wide open, searching for hope.

"That is our prayer. We hope and pray for the best. That's why I pray for you and make you say your prayers. I know it's hard to understand, but sometimes bad things happen to good people."

He nestled into her arms as he stared at the others watching the small black and white television.

A few weeks passed, and the usual routine of daydreaming at school and trying to come up with what he had learned was a habit. Stepping off the bus on this strange day, it just so happened that he was the only student at the stop.

Paul stood there all alone, then looked both ways before crossing. The only car he saw was far down the street, heading his way. He quickly ran across Ave E and arrived safely at the small church parking lot, where the walk home began. The same car he saw down the street was now slowly creeping to a stop several feet away.

He kept walking until a grown man, sitting in the back seat of the brown four-door car, shouted, "Hey, kid! Hold up a minute. I was wondering if you wanted this candy. We don't know what to do with it, but we thought you should have it."

With a thumping heart, his eyes quickly scanned the silhouettes of two men in the front seat. Also, a stringy brown-haired man, slightly balding with a huge mustache, was offering candy from the back passenger side window, holding out his cupped hands with a pile of a colorful assortment of sugary treats.

Paul's palms became sweaty as his hands slowly released his lunch box, and his other released his folder. With the sound of discarded school supplies, he shook his head slowly.

The man, dangling the candy, said, "Come on, we don't want it. Come and get it, kid!"

Their anger tipped, and the man fumed as he boldly hollered while getting out of the car. "Come here, kid!"

With a memory flash from the sheriff's story, Paul's image of the little blonde-haired girl with a white dress, and a sorrowful face, gripped him in fear. Within a split second, he bolted like the wind. His five-year-old legs flew with lightning speed, and he swore that superpowers flowed through his blood. Instead of escaping by the road, he chose to run through each of the four or five front yards.

A loud nuisance arose as he seemed to have awakened every dog. That was evident by excessive barking and clanking of assorted fences. He jumped over a railing of sorts and tumbled into the lawn. Soaring up and leaping around a birdbath, he then jumped over flowers. He darted through a row of hedges, feeling heavy scratches. *Don't turn around, don't turn around, keep running!*

Blasting through front yards seemed to repeat itself. It felt as though the few houses turned into a thousand. Finally, bursting through one more row of bushes, Paul fell into Johnny's long dirt drive, feeling every rock on his back while he tumbled. He leaped up and sprinted past Johnny's house and to the hedges.

Tears began to form, and the whole affair seemed like a nightmarish blur. All he could think about was jumping into his mother's arms, where it was safe.

Paul sprinted through the opening hedges, feeling giant hands would snatch him at any moment. He was relieved that the last steps to his house were clear of any obstacles.

Fleeing into his garage, he noticed a different car in his drive. Not caring who it belonged to, he flew through the breezeway and erupted into the dining room as Virginia jumped out of her chair. All Paul could see was his beautiful and safe mother, and he dove into her arms with a shower of tears and whaling fear. Her scent, her tight hold, gripped him in deep love, and his race felt over. A wave of danger seemed to lift as his heart bounced around his chest.

"Pauly, what happened? Why are you crying?" She looked over at her Avon lady, who was visiting.

He couldn't speak. He was out of breath.

"Oh my, he's bleeding. I hope everything is okay with Paul." The saleswoman stood.

Hearing a strange voice, Paul realized they were not alone, and a sudden wave of embarrassment began to creep in. Feeling the need for bravery, he stepped back and wiped away his tears. He looked at the lady and thought he did not mind his manners. But he had a tale to tell and quickly blurted out, "Bad men tried stealing me at the bus stop. The mean man in the back seat was holding candy out the window, and then he got mad and started to get out of the car, so I ran."

All color left Virginia's face as she cried, "Oh, Pauly, was there more than one? Good gracious."

She grabbed him tighter, smothering him.

The Avon lady gasped and covered her mouth.

Virginia blurted out, "I'm calling the sheriff. Here, you sit down and let me get a washcloth and some water. Where did you get those scratches?"

The Avon lady ran to the kitchen, and Virginia brought a wet cloth and washed his face. Reaching the rotary phone, she dialed the sheriff and asked them to come right away.

Kneeling and checking over his wounds, she asked, "What happened, you are filthy, and your shirt is torn. Did they hurt you?"

Paul shook his head. "I dropped my stuff and ran. But I ran through everyone's yard. I didn't look back, and I didn't want to run down the street. I didn't want them to catch me."

"Pauly!" She washed his arms. "You did the right thing."

The Avon lady handed him water and said, "Here, take a drink. You must have been very brave to run like that and get away."

Was I brave? he questioned himself, and then his eyes widened. "Mom... I was scared. This is the same story the sheriff told us in school. These bad guys were trying to steal me using candy."

"Well, thank God you're safe," she said, placing a calming hand on his cheek. "Again, you did the right thing."

After a short spell, Virginia looked out the front window. "Here comes the sheriff. Come on, Paul, you need to tell him everything."

The patrol car slowly approached, and the officer stepped out. They greeted him in the front yard. Virginia thanked the Avon lady, and she departed.

The officer bent to face Paul and smiled. "Hello, son. Can you tell me what happened?"

Paul stared at the sheriff's belt, which held his gun. He imagined that if he were a sheriff, he would have drawn the sidearm and shot at the bad guys.

"Son? Can you tell me about the incident?"

"Pauly, I know you're scared, but please tell the officer what happened."

Looking up at his mom, he began to tell his story and did not leave out any details. The officer nodded, and Paul didn't notice that he pulled out a notepad and wrote everything he said.

The sheriff said, "Wow, son, you did the right thing. Now, I would like to backtrack your every step, and we will go get your lunch pail. I think I saw it in the church parking lot when I drove by."

Paul's mind began to puff up with the thought that he was, indeed, a brave individual. He led them through the hedges to Johnny's house and into the neighbor's yard. They walked down the long drive as Cindy, the pony, neighed behind them in her corral.

He began feeling leadership as he directed the officer, showing every bush and fence he had jumped and or leaped through. Knowing very well, he learned these tactics from his older brothers, who, in his mind, were the bravest heroes he knew. These tactics were learned from playing army or running from the enemy. Pretending to fight and kick and swing weapons was their regular playtime routine. Paul always watched and looked up to his older brothers and would mimic their actions.

They finally reached the parking lot, and there sat his discarded lunch pail and folder. The friendly officer retrieved them for his mother.

Once again, bending down, the sheriff asked, "Can you describe the car and the men you saw? We need every detail if we are to catch them."

Pouring out every morsel of his young memory, the officer was pleased and complimented how observant he was. "This brown, four-door sedan is suspect. We have heard of this description before. Same with the mustache man you saw holding the candy. You have been a courageous and helpful young boy. I want you to know I am very proud of you." Turning to Virginia, he said, "You know, this means that we suggest that you meet him here from now on."

Nodding, she said, "I will. He usually has companions with him; this is the first time he was alone."

"That's interesting, which leads me to believe that these criminals, or dirt-bags, we like to call them, know the routes. They are probably watching and waiting for opportunities." The officer looked up and down the street.

"Wait a minute. You mean these men drive up and down our streets all of the time?" Virginia was mortified. *This trash is right outside my front door?*

She suddenly appreciated that the house was set far off the street. "Well, add this to my growing fears I have as a mother. I will tell my other five children the minute they get home."

"Sounds like you and your husband have your hands full."

"No, no husband, just me and my six children."

The officer was taken aback. "My apologies, but you are raising six children by yourself?"

Looking down at Paul, she said, "Nope, they all pitch in, and we do it together."

"Your mother is a strong woman, Paul. Now I know where your bravery comes from. Virginia, you make sure you spread the word to your neighbors if they have children as well. Keep them away from the street for now." The officer rubbed Paul's hair and suggested they head back and that their investigation was over.

Paul couldn't wait to tell his brothers and sisters. Walking back, a sense of pride arose as he watched his mother and finally really listened, for the first time, understanding that, indeed, she was brave. *I get it from my mother,* he thought.

He beamed and noticed how hard she worked for the family. That night, she sat by Paul's bed and answered Keith's many questions about the sheriff and then again about the bad guys. Mom looked tired, but she answered them all and noticed the rest of the kids were outside the door listening.

Speaking a little louder so they could all hear her, she said, "I am thankful to all of you. Keep an eye out for each other. And as you grow old, promise me you will always stay close. Don't be like those families that split apart and never talk to each other."

With hugs and kisses, and prayers, they went off to bed.

Paul lay there in the dark, replaying the dangerous tale repeatedly. He couldn't wait to wake up and tell it all again.

And those bad guys were never seen again.

Single Mom Six Kids & a Piano

Chapter 7

Cindy the Snapping Pony

On Betty's property, toward the back, was a large area that corralled Cindy, the snapping pony. Where did she get the snapping pony nickname? It was given to her by one of Virginia's kids. Which kid gave her this name? No one can recall.

The younger was terrified of the beast. Cindy had a knack for always revealing her mammoth teeth, followed by a snapping sound. It was probably normal for a pony but frightening for kids with enormous imaginations.

The surrounding fence was tall, and if Cindy saw you coming, she would quickly approach. Most likely, guessing food was involved. But if it wasn't, it didn't matter because she would still follow through with the usual ritual of brandishing those chompers. The biting would begin if any part of you dared cross her threshold, whether your body or even a finger.

One weekend day, Greg listened to his neighbor Johnny's grand and dangerous idea of climbing and playing with their G.I. Joe's high in the forbidden tree. What is the forbidden tree? It happened to be the only tree in the middle of the corral, where no kid dared enter. If you did, which no fool would even think about, it was for sure suicide to try and climb the tree.

"Well, what's your genius plan to get past Cindy? You brag as if it's easy." Greg looked over at the tree.

"My mom and dad are gone. They won't be back for a couple of hours. So, we have time. Now listen, we throw food way over at the far corner. See, over there!" He pointed. "We chuck it on the ground and slowly walk away. When her head is down, you know, scarfing it up, we run back here and leap the gate. Then we climb. She will never see us. Can you dig it or what?"

"That's your dumb idea?" After many failed plans and adventures in the past with Johnny, one including painful stitches and who could forget biting Brutus in the foxhole, Greg's suspicions peaked. "I don't know…it could keep her distracted?"

After a long pause and tempting climbing bliss, he looked around for any grownup to thwart their plans. Finally, glancing into their pack, full of G.I. Joe's, he knew the tree would be a great and thrilling, high-altitude adventure for his toys. So, he gave the nod.

Greg opened the side gate to the stable. Johnny darted in, taking a scoop of feed. He held up the grub, showing Greg the pony's tasty morsels. "She digs this junk."

He sped off to the distant corner, dumped the food, and called her name. Watching as the plan fell into place perfectly, they acted cool as they slowly walked away, whistling, with hands in their pockets.

"Well, to the tree, we finally go!" Johnny shouted.

Greg told him to shut up and not give them away. This was it. The first time he was braving and daring to enter the corral of danger, followed by the unthinkable and the never-before climbing the forbidden tree.

They scurried over the wooden gate and jumped to the ground. Hearing their thud, Cindy turned. As the brave warriors sprinted to the tree, Cindy's crazy eyes flamed, and her fierce anger launched. She neighed, galloping toward them, furious that someone dared enter her space.

With adrenaline pumping, Greg blew past Johnny and soared to the first branch, then the second. Johnny shrieked as the distraught pony suddenly appeared. He frantically grabbed the first branch and flew to the second as Greg watched from his high perch.

Cindy's predictable teeth were in clear view as she began snapping at Johnny's hind end. He yelled as he survived the menacing chompers.

Greg grabbed Johnny's arm, hoisted him up, and they shouted in triumph.

The victory was theirs as Johnny taunted, "Not fast enough, are you...stupid pony?"

Laughter reigned as the pony circled her tree. This new threat seemed to ignite her rage. What was worse, they completely ignored her, and somehow, she knew it.

They climbed to the highest branches, feeling like they were on top of the world. Looking through the clearing, Johnny pointed to their treehouse to the southwest. Greg's house was visible, and the adjacent field was too.

"This is far out. I dig this view!" Greg laughed.

Johnny agreed. "Everything looks so different from higher up."

Finding a thick branch to play on without losing their stuff, they pulled out the G.I. Joe's, and the military sorties launched. Explosions and screams echoed as soldiers battled and raged from on top of the world. After playing for an hour, their fun halted as a sudden realization of building a grand treehouse began. Ideas for the floor plan unfolded, and both were calling out the different rooms needed. Such as food storage, bedrooms, restrooms, and a string line, can-to-can string phone service was included.

There was nothing in their way imagining this magnificent tree palace until Greg blurted out, "I gotta take a wiz!"

Johnny snapped from his construction trance and said, "Well, then go."

"From up here? I don't want to wiz on Cindy. She'd be double mad. Besides, I'm starving. I want food."

Greg scanned his roof again, wondering if his mom had made dinner yet as the sun began to set. "So, what's your plan to get Cindy to scram so we can split?"

Johnny looked befuddled as he glanced down at the pacing pony. "Shucks, I haven't thought of that. Do I have to think of everything? Listen, you jerk, you could have made plans!"

"She's your stupid pony, just like your idiot dog. This is just swell; we are living the fox-hole caper all over again? I knew this was a bad idea, and my mom says to never trust you ever since you whacked me in the head with that hoe! I should've listened. Now I am going to get eaten by a mad pony. Just swell, Johnny, I give you the doofus award."

Greg began to descend.

"Listen, bub. You want to get clobbered again? I don't care what your mom says!"

Greg's fiery eyes blazed. "You…clobber me? In your dreams, you twerp. If you dare say anything about my mom, I'll pound you. Why don't you clobber your stupid animal and get her to leave? Just so maybe, maybe, we can escape without bleeding."

The lower they climbed it seemed like a magnet to Cindy. They climbed higher, she walked away, they came down, and she was below. Frustration ruled, but they realized they both needed a truce and came together for a sufficient escape plan.

Greg said, "Well, Einstein, we can go run at the same time. I jump here, and you jump there, maybe it will confuse her, and she only chases one of us?"

"That's so stupid. I'll scream for help. Maybe my dad will hear me."

"What an idiot, just like the foxhole? Your dumb screaming got us nowhere last time and only hurt my ears. What a great plan. Besides, you said your parents were gone. And let's say your dad was here and did hear you, then what, he whips us? What's worse, Cindy biting us or a whipping?"

Johnny thought hard about it. "Man, you have a point." Panic-stricken, he said, "Okay, we jump on three. Oh boy, this is gunna hurt."

They dropped to the lower branches, Greg on one side and Johnny farther away. Cindy was confused and randomly paced.

"Alright, I'll count," Greg said. "One, two, three!"

Leaping down, Cindy chose to charge Greg as he bolted for the gate.

Don't look back, don't look back! Thoughts of gnarly, piercing teeth freaked him out as his legs burned and his bladder pressed.

Hoofs thumped closer, and seeing the nearing gate, Greg had yet to receive any bites, to his surprise.

His high adrenaline ignited his muscles as he jumped with all his might. He managed to leap over the gate. Feeling like superman and flying over the top horizontal boards with no bites, he felt freedom was near. Until he quickly realized what lay dead ahead: he was careening toward the pecan tree and a metal water spigot.

Crash!

His leg slammed the metal pipe, sending him tumbling to a painful stop. Grabbing his bleeding shin, he rolled in agony, seeing flesh, and watching the blood pour through his now torn pants.

Greg groaned some more and kept watching the blood, wondering when Johnny would leap the fence.

As the pain subsided, he slowly lifted himself. Hobbling to the gate, he sluggishly climbed, looking for traces of Johnny's scattered remains. All he saw was Cindy, now standing under the tree. No blood, no half-eaten Johnny.

Greg scanned left to the far fence, but no Johnny. He looked right toward home; no one rustled in the hedges.

"My gosh, did she eat him!" The disgusting visual horrifically played in his mind as he imagined her swallowing him whole.

He looked at her belly to see if Johnny was wiggling inside. Thoughts of Little Red Riding Hood ran through his mind. *I'll need Patrick's help with slicing Cindy open to free Johnny. That's gross and cool at the same time.*

Suddenly, Johnny's voice rang out, "Hey Greg, nice leap. You must have flown six feet in the air to clear the gate. That was cool!"

Looking around for his distant voice, he found Johnny hanging on the lower branch, still in the tree.

"I got scared and figured you can help me after you get out. So, here is my better idea, can you lure Cindy into the stall and lock the gate behind her? What do you know, maybe we should have done that in the first place?"

Greg stared forever while his leg throbbed and bled. "Goodbye, Johnny!"

Stepping down and limping away, he heard Johnny's fading voice yelling and pleading for help. "That chump can rot up there, he mumbled."

Thus ended the great forbidden tree caper.

Chapter 8

Oak Glen and Thurman Flat

The year was 1971, and Apollo 14 landed on the moon for the 3rd successful mission with astronaut Alan Shepard. The first Soviet space station, called Salyut 1, launched. The latest toys invented were the Etch-a-Sketch and the buzzing game Operation. Women were finally allowed to vote in Switzerland, and the Amtrak trains were created.

Virginia, not owning a car, had difficulty getting around town. She had a deep desire to make sure her children attended church. One Sunday, while walking to church, Virginia met a dear lady named Ann. Ann was thin with a warm smile. She was a senior citizen with gentle wrinkles and gray hair. She gracefully dressed, always wore a bumper-style hat, and was willing to drive the troops to church every Sunday. Her 1950 blue Chevy Impala arrived for the first time, and the kids were in awe at the pristine car.

"She must be rich!" Cynthia blurted.

A stern warning came from Virginia as they entered. The kids sat quietly as their mom and the dear saint conversed. The ride was short.

"We're so thankful for the lift." Virginia stepped out.

Ann looked at the children warmly and said, "You all meet me here after church. Maybe, just maybe, your mother will agree for us all to go for a little drive afterward. You kids deserve it because you are so well-behaved."

Virginia glanced at her children, and Maureen answered, "Thank you very much for the nice compliment."

This made Virginia beam as she went off to find a seat.

Virginia saw an empty row. She entered, and the kids followed. They sat properly. The kids were taught how to conduct themselves in church and never complain—no fidgeting, no squirming, and for sure, no giggling. Mass took forever for the younger, they found it hard to sit still, but they did what they were told, with no exceptions.

Once Mass was over, they all met at the car and politely piled in.

Ann asked Virginia, "Have you ever been around Hog Canyon and up and around Oak Glen? It only takes about fifteen minutes. And I do love a Sunday drive."

She stared at her children, their eyes shouting, *yes*!

Virginia answered, "We've lived here for several years now but don't get out much. We would love the drive. The kids have never been to Oak Glen, but I have, so many years ago, and would like to see it again."

"Good, they will love it," Ann said, turning left on California street.

Ann lowered her window to catch the tasteful fall air. With an eagerness to cruise the canyon and excitement to finally see Oak Glen, they motored up the road with the wind wrapping their faces. The canyon was narrow with a grove of live oak. They were full and mature, and the dry grasses swayed like luring hands, waving them to come and play.

A park came into view, and the road was an adventure with three separate dips that excited everyone's stomachs. The first dip was minimal, the second raised laughter, and the deepest one caused a collective *yelp!*

The car dropped down and rambled through. Laughter and peering heads abounded as they dubbed Wildwood Canyon Rd, *The Dips*.

Immediately ascending out of the drop, they climbed into a canopy of oaks to higher ground.

It felt like an ascension to the top of the world as they could see for miles. Far away, the San Jacinto Mountain range reached the clouds. Empty meadows and wide-open landscapes covered everywhere their eyeballs scanned. At the stop sign, the road choices were down to Cherry Valley or climbing north to see the face of the towering San Gorgonio mountains. They looked alive, rising high and ominous.

As Ann motored up the mountain, many eyes stared, pointing and gawking at the steep mountain terrain. She then slowed her car on the only saddle of the road. The kids looked down both sides into the canyon below, and Ann checked her mirrors and stopped the vehicle.

Virginia, puzzled, looked around and asked, "Is everything all right."

"Yes, it is. This is *Gravity Hill*. Well, that's what we call it," Ann said, pointing to the road they were stopped on. "See out the front window. We are facing downhill. Now you kids, see how we are heading down this road; watch as I put the car in neutral and see what happens."

Once she did so, the car began to roll backward up the hill, to their amazement. The kids were like caged birds looking everywhere, trying not to touch the glass.

Patrick couldn't help it. He blurted, "This is so cool!"

Greg followed with, "Far out!"

Ann stopped, dropped the car in drive, and continued up the road, and the kids were abuzz with whispers of how they appeared to be coasting uphill.

Virginia and Ann began to converse again, and the kids loved every mile of the Sunday drive. As they climbed the last hill lined with yellow trees, the old stone schoolhouse came into view. Around the hairpin was the beginning of small shops, and there was a vast lawn to cartwheel on or play tag…well, maybe just cartwheels if Virginia had her say.

The climbing and sloping apple groves were abundant. Dreamful cabins and a few modern homes rested on both sides of the road, and all imagined moving there right away.

Before they knew it, a small village came into view. A tall A-frame building and a fenced outside area along the road were first.

"Kids, look at the deer in the pin." Virginia pointed.

The car seemed to lean to the right as they all pushed to see the animals. As the car eased around the bend, the entire village opened up, and it felt like they were in a different world. There was a line of knick-knack shops, a bakery, and a restaurant.

Virginia pointed again. "Is that the old candy store?"

"Yes, they have plenty of chocolates and caramel apples. And the biggest pickle barrel I have ever seen. Up further, they even have a self-guided pathway to see a variety of animals if you ever want to take your children. It does cost, though," Ann said as she kept driving.

The kids were eager to explore this mini-Disneyland of the mountains, but their excitement began to deflate as the car slowly passed the shops.

As if feeling the same vibe, Virginia blurted, "Can you pull in?"

Ann grinned and replied, "I'm glad you want to. You won't be disappointed."

She turned into the driveway, and they pulled in front of the candy store. Towering trees and concrete stairs welcomed them inside.

Just as Ann had said, they were not disappointed. Aromas of chocolate and warm caramel lured them closer. Everywhere they looked was candy euphoria. Baskets of lollipops, barrels of candies, and glass cases with various kinds of chocolates stared back. Licorice and hard candies were on display all around; the kids had never seen anything like it. They had to suppress their desires because, first, Virginia never allowed them to touch anything, and second, they didn't have any money.

Patrick waved everyone over to a large wooden barrel. Looking inside, they saw that it was full of the most gigantic pickles that ever existed. Paul had to have help to see over the edge, and Keith was on his tippy toes. Staring at the hundred swimming pickles, they marveled and wondered what giant land they came from. Even those who didn't like pickles wanted to chomp into them right away.

Cynthia yelled, "Look at the taffy stretcher!"

The colorful arrangement was like an artist's tapestry.

To add to their sweet intoxication, Maureen summoned the troops to watch the workers turn chocolate, drooling over what it would be like to chew each piece. The older kids lifted Keith and Paul, and they couldn't even imagine that so much chocolate was on planet earth. Their heads were dizzy with sugary aromas and overload, but they knew it was not affordable.

The chocolate artisans had a tight grip on the sizeable hypnotic spoon while masterfully stirring the cauldron of happiness. Its spell possessed the onlookers until their mother said, "Kids, you can pick out one candy, and I will buy it for you."

The children checked their ears as Virginia's words slowly registered. Their hearts were raised in warm appreciation, and they humbly questioned if they could afford it. Maureen, being the oldest, knew it was a sacrifice.

But Greg quickly questioned the impossibilities of the offer and said, "Just one? One candy…that's impossible."

The older kids laughed.

Keith and Paul stared at each other with colossal smiles. They suddenly floated toward the chocolate displays. Staring hard and pointing to their choices, they both agreed to choose the chocolate-covered, peanut butter rectangle things. They couldn't name them; being lost in their sweet draw, they could only dumbly point toward the chocolate of their choice. Their world went silent as they observed the clerk reach in and bag their delectable morsels. Their mouths watered as they imagined what it would taste like.

Knowing they were moments away from chomping into their delights, Virginia paid, held the bags, and looked down. "We need to wait until we get home."

To their dismay, they felt the floor begin to swallow them alive. *Home, what?*

They silently and collectively groaned but knew better not to complain.

Their light in the darkness came when Ann said, "I'm in no hurry if you're not, Virginia. I want to eat my honeycomb now. You know, eat it while it's fresh. We can walk around a bit if you want?"

Virginia looked at the eager, dessert-famished faces. "Well, I'm sure it won't hurt one time if we eat dessert before our meal. Kids, would you like to eat your candy now?"

With an atomic blast of hands and jumping, the kids leaped as they shouted, "Yes!"

The time warp that followed even stunned the kids. It seemed as quickly as they had received their candy, it disappeared even more quickly. The grins on their faces were widespread because the candy was a delight. The surprise of a Sunday drive to Oak Glen was even more over the top than they had imagined.

Virginia made sure they were squeaky clean before entering the car.

They arrived home, and the kids piled out, excited for the Sunday drive.

Ann offered, "Next week, maybe we can have a picnic at Thurman Flat? What do you say, Virginia?"

Glancing at their faces and seeing how much fun they had, Virginia felt guilty that she couldn't take them anywhere, let alone afford it. But a picnic, that was easy. She answered, "Well, I don't see why not. But what or where is a Thurman Flat?"

"Oh, good. I will keep it a surprise. It is close, and you and your family will love it." She waved and drove away.

The kids had a blast sharing their likes about the candy store, and if they had oodles of money, they knew where they would go.

That night after dinner, Cynthia snuggled in. "Mom, Yucaipa really is a beautiful place. We live so near to the mountains. Can we visit the candy store again?"

"I don't see why not. Someday we'll have transportation, and if we save our money for a special trip, we will. Let's pray that I can afford a car. That's a good place to start."

"Ann is very nice, isn't she?" Cynthia asked while Maureen nodded in agreement.

"Very nice…and brave. Anyone who would allow seven passengers in their car is brave." Virginia chuckled.

Maureen replied, "And the boys didn't even break anything."

"If they did, I would wring their necks! Now, off to bed, girls. Good night." Virginia kissed them on their heads, and off they went.

Overhearing the last part of the conversation, Keith yelled from his bed, "What does wring your neck mean?"

Paul rose with interest.

"You boys should be asleep," Virginia said.

"We keep talking about the candy store," Keith answered. "So, what does wring your neck mean?"

"In the old days on the farm, when they wanted a chicken dinner, they would chase their chickens, catch'm, and wring their necks. Snapping it, you know, killing it."

The boys felt their necks with wrenched faces.

"Then, they would cut off its head and drain the blood. Now, off to bed and sweet dreams."

Keith said, "That's cool. Can we get chickens?"

"Go to sleep, and no more talking." Virginia closed their door, and the whispers now went on about chickens.

The week flew by, and Sunday rolled around, and Anne gathered the troops and drove them to church. The kids didn't show it, but they were dancing a jig inside because they knew they were going on a picnic. A picnic just sounded magical by itself. First, you have the basket, which seemed to burst with your food and beverage likings. Second, the picnic area was like an extension of a basket, full of all the outdoor likings, such as trees, a vast sky, and climbable things. However, filling a magical wicker basket with a handle and two flaps on the top was something Virginia couldn't do because she didn't own one. So, in this case, an affordable small cardboard box and a brown bag would suffice.

The box was filled with sandwiches and chips and a thermos with powdered lemonade. Knowing you get to eat somewhere outside was kids' heaven. Even Virginia loved the great outdoors, and any chance she could find to travel into God's creation was great therapy.

Leaving the church, they drove to Hwy 38 and turned right. The kid's eyes were again peeled, taking in every visual detail of the mouth of Mill Creek Canyon as they headed up the road.

Driving over the bridge, Patrick yelled, "There's a river down there!"

"Patrick, mind your manners. No yelling in the car," Virginia sternly rebuked.

"Sorry, Mother," he returned.

Ann, in her truly kind way, said, "Virginia, I don't mind if the kids are excited. I mean, look at this place."

"It's pretty, and I can't believe it's so close to home. We haven't even been driving for ten minutes, and there's already such beauty to take in." Virginia beamed.

"Did you kids know that this canyon is an earthquake fault?" Ann glanced in her rear-view mirror as their eyes lit up.

Virginia answered, "So this canyon is the San Andreas Fault I have heard about?"

"It sure is. Do you kids still want to picnic?" Ann laughed as the kids gave their usual, *far-out,* and *cool.*

Pulling into the campground of Thurman Flat, the entrance dipped down, and they parked. The canopy of alders and live oak lined the sky, and boulders peeked through the thick vines. To the left were stone walls and a landing with tables. The children wanted to dash into the woods, but their mother laid down the rules before they could. "Ann says these vines are blackberries, and there is a trail straight through to the water. Go play, and you watch out for Keith and Pauly. Be back in a half-hour, and lunch will be ready."

They sped off through the narrow trail. The forest floor was thick with berry vines and fallen branches, and they could hear the roar of the creek nearby. Stepping over small streams and seeing old berries was exciting. Sunrays sent fingers of light through the thick branches, and the scent of wet soil and foliage drifted by.

The siblings reached the water; it looked inviting and clear. Cupping their hands, four sipped and slurped, and Maureen thought they were gross.

Finding stones to leap across, Greg made it first, followed by Patrick. To their amazement, they arrived at the immense boulder they had ever seen. The massive rock lay there like it was out of place. The rock was too large for Keith and Paul, so they went to the water's edge to build roads and buildings.

"Where did this even come from?" Patrick asked. "Let's climb it."

After several tries, they ascended five to six feet before leaping back down, and before they knew it, Maureen announced that it was time for lunch.

"Ah, man!" Keith and Paul yelled as their mini-construction sight abruptly ended, but not before smashing it to bits.

Cynthia tossed rocks in the creek and laid down her finely chosen stones.

Marching in a single line, like in a fairy tale, while some were whistling, they arrived at the picnic table, and the food spread was enticing. Sandwiches, fruit, chips, cookies, and canned olives grabbed their appetite. They quickly sat, and their hunger notched up ten-fold.

Virginia smiled at their excitement and was thrilled to be able to provide a picnic treat with Ann's help, who she thought was a true saint.

"Let's say grace before we eat," Virginia said.

The prayers of thankfulness reached God's throne, and the kids thought everything tasted better outdoors. Virginia used the can opener and partly opened the metal olive lid. Peeling it open but not completely cutting it all the way. This method was to push the lid closed later. "Now, the lid is very sharp, don't cut yourself on it. Be careful."

Passing the olives, they had to portion them. When the can reached Paul, on cue, he grabbed it and felt a strange sensation. He sat there, trying to dump some olives, blood dripped from his thumb. Yep, he cut himself. Staring at his deep cut, he said, "Mommy, I cut myself."

As he announced his wound, he stared across the table at Cynthia as the sides of his eyes blackened, and he fell into a darkened world. Of course, down he went, sinking backward off the bench onto the grassy floor, and he was out for the count. The buzz around the table was that the olive can had won that round.

Paul slowly began to open his eyes, and there above him was an angel who descended from above, encouraging him with words of comfort. The angel spoke, "Pauly, didn't I tell you to watch out for the lid? You passed out. I guess you are one of those kids that accidents seem to follow. Let's get you up. I have band-aids."

Beads of sweat dripped down his face as he felt woozy. The gang wanted to see the cut, and Paul didn't dare look again. "What happened?" he slurred.

"Oh Pauly, not only are you susceptible to passing out, but you're also becoming accident-prone." Virginia shook her head.

The food was obliterated, much to everyone's enjoyment. No leftovers to be seen, except a few bloodstained olives, which were tossed.

The charge went out for the kids to go and play one more time, but Pauly had to stay put, much to his disliking.

"Virginia, how do you like Thurman Flat?" Ann asked.

"It's just what we needed. It's beautiful, and again, I can't believe it's so close to home. Really, we live in a wonderful town. Thank you, Ann. We really appreciate it. You truly are kind to help us."

"Well, the Lord helped me, and I help you. I will be glad to drive you to church until the Lord provides for you a car. Does that sound like a deal?"

"It's a deal. May I give you gas money?"

"I wouldn't take it. Besides, I like your children. You are an amazing woman and doing a marvelous job raising them. They are so well-mannered. Truly, the Lord has blessed you."

Feeling worn out all the time, Virginia laughed. "Thank you, I do have my doubts sometimes, but I'm grateful. Ann, there is a favor to ask. I've been given a job interview for Lockheed in Mentone. Would you be able to drive me? I know it's asking a lot."

"Good for you. It would be my pleasure." Ann smiled.

"Now that Pauly is in school, I think I can wing it and hopefully have a little more spending money."

Chapter 9

The Bel-Air

The year was 1972, and Lockheed was awarded a significant contract for the new space-shuttle program. America had designed a reusable shuttle on print only, and it was in the beginning phase of the next chapter in the space race. Its purpose, galactic studies, and the new conceptual space station.

Virginia was hired as an administrative assistant in Lockheed's library, which was used for archiving and engineering studies. She was excited and took to it quickly. She enjoyed having a routine to build her skills for future employment.

Speeding to the bus stop and walking as fast as her heels allowed, she barely made it. She sat and huffed, trying to catch her breath. The bus jerked and bounced, jostling her breakfast and coffee.

"Shame, isn't it?" A man's voice echoed from across the aisle. "Did you hear there was a terrorist attack in Munich? It's a darn shame what is happening in our world. And if that is not bad enough, I think ole Nixon is going to get himself in trouble." He turned and buried his head back in the daily paper.

Still, out of breath, Virginia looked out her window and thought about what was outside of her home. The big world and the big picture. Mostly sheltered from it, she hadn't put much thought into what was happening outside her sphere; daily survival always ruled her waking moments. *The world...what will it be like when my kids grow? What have I brought them into? God, I pray they have a fighting chance at living a good and Godly life. Please, guide their path, and make it vastly different from my own. I pray they have easier lives.*

She stared out the bus window.

After arriving at work, she sat behind her typewriter. Shoving her purse into the lower desk drawer, she reached for her shorthand notepad. Cheerfully she settled in, and hunger for improving her skill dominated.

Hours later, she slid the notepad aside and spied the clock. Lunch break would be practice time. But for now, the Lockheed library had books that needed attending. To finally start earning an income made her happy. *It may not be much, but a job is a job! As long as my foot is in the door, there is hope for upward promotions.*

Every time she walked by the secretaries, she dreamed of the day that would be her. Salaries could certainly be boosted if she worked in that position. Searching and striving to find an edge in helping to better herself was in sight. Virginia was beyond grateful that she took her mother's advice to learn shorthand. Having this skill was her hope of tipping her above the rest. *Oh, Virginia, probably everyone else is learning it better than you. Well, I have to try!*

The daily wrestling continued.

Her fingers glided across the sleek IBM typewriter as stillness busied around her. Pausing, she took in an incredible silence. She closed her eyes and whispered, "Peace and quiet will do me some good."

She got up, filed the returned books, and organized the disorder. Her eyes fixed on straightening the chairs around the tables. Soon, the break-buzzer hummed; it was time to meet her co-workers, who were headed for the break room for the much-desired coffee.

Virginia poured herself a cup, and she stretched her aching back. *Most likely from my inferior mattresses and couch sleeping excursions,* she thought.

A tall, fashion magazine-type woman with blonde and what Virginia considered perfect hair appeared and immediately approached. Her blue eyes were bright, but her smirk wasn't pleasant.

Fiddling with her coffee cup, she stared and said, "So, you're Virginia? I heard they filled the library position. I'm Mary, and it's nice to meet you. I'm a secretary, one of the busy bees out there in the hive." She pointed to the large room with several desks piled together. "Don't worry. You will get used to us. We like to gab…" She chuckled as she looked around. "Just don't gab in front of the bosses. They frown at that."

Virginia finished her sip and cautiously said, "Nice to meet you, Mary. How long have you been with Lockheed?"

"I've been here, let's see, going on three years." Stirring her creamer, she added, "I see you are not wearing a wedding ring, so I assume you are not married. Are you still looking for Mr. Right?"

"No," Virginia answered quickly. "I stay busy enough."

A flush of anger crept over her from this question, and a sense of secrecy rushed through her mind. *The last thing I want is my life to be out there for their next gab session.*

Wanting the conversation to be over before any more questions could be asked, Virginia said, "Nice to meet you." And she headed for the outside patio area.

Many were smoking, sitting, and jabbering about current events. The break was over while she paced back and forth, trying to work the kinks out of her back.

Virginia headed back to her duties. With the help of coffee, her morning tasks were completed, and the work was enjoyable.

For so long, Virginia had felt guilty for not being able to bring in money for her family. However, feeling her worth, earning money, and not being dependent began to relieve some of that guilt. Taking something for nothing had never sat well in her heart.

Thinking back years ago about her last employment, it was at the Long Beach shipyards. Once again, after her first real paycheck, albeit small, a sensation of an excellent first step to independence was fulfilling. But weighing the dollar amount against buying food, shoes, clothing, medicine, and paying the usual bills seemed daunting. Rolling her eyes, she mumbled, "It's a start Virginia, it's a start."

On her way to the bus stop after work, she saw that the bench was empty. The bus soon arrived, and after stepping on, a vain hope ensured Virginia that her co-workers didn't notice. Being impoverished ate at her conscience, and dread followed. The truth was, being monetarily poor was the swirling reality. Often swelling of pride would arise in her heart. At the same time, she would fight to extinguish it and find the area of thankfulness.

She took to the window seat and stared out. *I sure wish I had a car.*

A sense of embarrassment tugged at her heart as the battle of her thoughts continued.

Sudden memories of the past rolled in of when she used to own a sleek convertible, MG. While the bus rambled on and she watched the road, recollections sailed her to when she was still single and had the top down, cruising down the Pacific Coast Highway. She closed her eyes and tried to remember.

Virginia imagined the waves crashing on the beach, the wind blowing her hair, and the salty air causing a delightful smile. She pulled in for a treat with the Pike in Long Beach in view. Ordering a malt, she sat back in her cool, convertible beauty. She sipped the chocolatey goodness, then continued for a sunset cruise down PCH.

The jolt from the bus snapped her back to reality. "At least you have a job now and a way to get to work, be thankful," she said under her breath as she let out a long sigh. *Let it go, Virginia. Those memories were a long time ago.*

Several months passed, and the job groove felt easier. A sense of pride in being a librarian arose since she was now walking in her mother's footsteps.

On a Saturday morning, the phone rang.

"Mom, you have a phone call!" Maureen yelled to the outside, where Virginia was speaking to the Wheelers.

"If you will excuse me, nice talking to you." She headed back and handed Maureen a smooth and beautiful cut rock. "It's a gift from our neighbor. Who's on the phone?"

"Aunt Joyce."

She took the phone and said, "Hello?"

Maureen stared at the long pause.

"Are you kidding?" Virginia continued, "This is, this is, oh, I'm stumped for words. Joyce, thank you. This will change our world. Today? You're coming by today? What time?"

Another pause hovered as Maureen squeezed in to overhear the conversation. *What is so great?* she wondered.

"Okay, please tell them that I'm very grateful, and can I give a few dollars? I don't have much." Another long pause. "Free, my golly, thank you, yes, thank you, okay, okay, see you soon."

Click.

Virginia hung up the phone and stared into Maureen's eyes. With a smile as wide as could be, she grabbed Maureen's arms. "Our prayers have been answered. We are getting a free car!"

Jumping up and down with excitement, the rest of the mob gathered for the proclamation of rare, good news. Every bit of that good news was spread quickly through the household. Cheers and laughter bounced off the windows until Virginia saw Maureen's sudden, long face. "What is it?"

"Can we afford it? I mean, gas? Can we afford to have a car?"

What Maureen said quieted the crowd, and they all stared from Maureen to Mom, wondering if this dream couldn't come true.

"Yes, the car is free, my brother can help if something breaks, and we will only drive it when we need to. But, for sure, we will take this offer. It will be here in an hour."

Cheers rocketed once more.

The youngest eagerly waited, perking up every time a car drove by. The oldest ran down the driveway and stood by the curb. Great anticipation soared for just a glimpse.

"Now, Maureen, brace yourself. It's an old car, from Joyce's description. It sounded like they were going to throw it away. So, the owner's grandkids began thrashing it. When Uncle Andy saw this, he quickly stopped them and mentioned our need for a car. They agreed, so it may not be a looker, but it runs, and beggars can't be choosers."

"What kind of car is it?" Cynthia asked.

"She said a Bel-Air Chevy; I think 1959. That's all I know."

Soon enough, a ruckus was heard outside, and the kids ran alongside a car, barreling up the long drive. It was a faded white machine with a tattered headrest flapping ghostly in the wind.

Virginia was humbled and awestruck that she was thought of. Most of all, it was free. She hugged her brother-in-law, and soon her sister and her kids pulled up behind.

"This is wonderful, Andy!"

She ran her hand down the side trim and looked inside. The kids began pouring in and out of the back seat, rolling up and down windows and cranking every knob they could find. Patrick turned the steering wheel left and right when a sudden shock ran through everyone as Greg smashed the horn. Laughing, Virginia furrowed her eyebrows at him.

Virginia turned to Andy and stated, "I have duct tape for the headrest. Could you help, Andy?"

"Sure thing, Pat, Greg, go get the tape and help me with the job."

Andy sat back in the car and began pulling the draping headrest and dislodging off the dangling pieces. The ripping tape sound ended, and Andy said, "There, good as new. Well, glistening gray if you don't mind the color."

"I love it!" Virginia sat behind the wheel. "Thanks again. This will be so helpful for work. I don't have to take the bus anymore. I can now run errands. Imagine something as simple as stopping and picking up milk on the way home will change our world. Really, we are very thankful and blessed that you were thinking of us."

She stepped out and embraced him.

He grinned. "Glad you're happy, Virginia. Now Joyce and I can save money on gas, not having to rush your kids to the hospital every week," Andy joked.

Great laughter erupted as Virginia concurred with the truth of his statement. They lived in Redlands, and Virginia had called on them so many times, and they faithfully came.

"I heard gas is supposed to stay steady at thirty-six cents a gallon. I hope it doesn't change."

"I hope it stays at that price, too. It still seems so expensive," Joyce replied.

Uncle Andy and his family said their goodbyes and headed home. Virginia waved and wore a huge smile, and as she turned around, six children were bobbing up and down like little eager toys. All were wearing the look of, *Please take us for a ride.*

She laughed. "Let me guess. You want to go for a ride in our new car?"

Screams and cheers burst as they all piled in and found their favorite spots. Cynthia sat in the middle of the front seat, and Maureen to her right. Patrick sat behind Maureen at the window seat, and Greg, Paul, and Keith sat behind Mom.

Paul immediately began to cry because he wanted to sit behind Mom by the window and would not have it any other way. Mom returned with her purse and ordered Keith to move.

Keith shoved Paul. "You're such a baby."

Paul sneered and didn't care. He got what he wanted, which was to be behind Mom. There were no seatbelt laws at the time, and they never wore them. So, since he was tiny, Paul scooted close to the back of his mom's seat and had the best view see over the top of the door.

Firing up the motor, Virginia pulled out and headed down the drive, and the kids were elated. They felt a richness. For the first time in this new adventurous life, they had a car.

Pulling left, shouts of probable destinations poured from the backseat. With all windows down, the mother and her six children let the wind blow through their hair. A quietness settled in as they enjoyed a ride in their car.

Toward the end of the drive, Virginia surprised them as the car wheeled into the local drive-through dairy on California Street. The kids were stunned when their mom ordered six small chocolate milk containers. After paying the man, everyone celebrated as they popped the lids and began to guzzle. These were great memories for them all.

Chapter 10

Sara, the Talking Car

Still, in 1972, Virginia was walking down the row of books marked *Engineering*. She put the hardbacks in their place and turned them right side up. A sudden clearing of a throat made her jump. Spinning around quickly, she saw a handsome man with dark, neatly trimmed hair, sideburns, and a thick mustache.

He chuckled. "I'm sorry, didn't mean to startle you."

"Oh, my apologies, I'm not used to this much quiet. Everything makes me jump." She headed for the desk.

Pulling a book from the shelf, he approached and said, "My name is Charlie. Nice to meet you, Virginia. I work over in the machine shop. Mary told me your name." He set the book down and glanced out the window.

Suddenly Virginia became aware of her appearance. *Is my hair okay?* She slowly propped the left curls. *He's not wearing a wedding ring.*

A nervous blush rose on her cheeks. *Good gracious, Virginia, get it together. He's just checking out a book!*

At that exact time, they both said, "Nice weather, we are…"

Charlie stopped and smiled, and Virginia looked down in embarrassment. "Ladies first." He laughed.

"I was saying what nice weather we are having." Her cheeks felt hot, and her countenance foolish.

She was so embarrassed that she would even have this feeling in her being. *Where were these silly feelings hiding?* she thought.

"I agree. Thanks for the book. I hope the knowledge in this book explains the mathematical equations to build the parts we need." Smiling and nodding, he walked out as she stared.

"The mathematical what? What is in these books? I guess Lockheed has this library for a reason. It's not like Dr. Suess' books."

She stood and walked to the window. "Anyway, what a nice gentleman," she whispered.

Virginia grabbed her purse and hurried to the restroom. Looking in the mirror at her hair, she frowned. Several flyways immediately stood out.

She laughed at her reflection. "Give it up, Virginia. You haven't a chance, nor should you even be thinking about it. You're not even divorced yet, and my kids would eat him alive."

The wind escaped her lungs with a strange hurt. She didn't know whether to laugh or cry; this was something not much attention was paid to. *I'm just surviving.*

Quickly, the word divorce strangled her like a noose draining hope of a boyfriend, let alone a new husband. *God, I'm sorry if my thoughts are wrong…please forgive me. I can't date or even think of another man. Guide me, please…I shouldn't be feeling this way.*

Virginia went back to work. So many thoughts ran through her mind when the lunch bell sounded. She picked up her sack lunch and headed outside to the small lawn and found a lone table. This, to her, was tradition. She had been keeping to herself for fear of becoming the center of gossip. Privacy mattered; it was instilled in her since childhood. *It's nobody's business what goes on in our personal lives*, Frankie taught her.

As she took a first large bite of her sandwich, a voice said, "May I join you?"

She jumped out of her seat and almost choked, seeing Charlie again.

"I'm sorry, that's twice now I scared you. May I sit?"

With a mouth full, she mumbled, "*Yes.*"

Nervous, she began wondering if she had food on her face or between her teeth. The sudden interest flustered her, and she realized it was so foreign. Bashfully looking away, she hurried to choke down her mouthful.

Virginia was confused that she unknowingly took another huge bite. Once again, a realization hit that her mouth was jammed packed, leaving no room for words and sending waves of embarrassment.

Smiling, Charlie followed suit, and they sat in the quiet and ate until completion.

"Well, Charlie, like anyone, I was starving." Virginia's nerves swirled as she screamed on the inside. *Starving, starving? That's all you can come up with?*

"Me too. Hey, I noticed you're driving a Bel-Air. I love old cars, and I mean that in a good way. They don't make'm like they used to."

Thankful for the change in subject, she replied, "Yes, it gets me from here to there. Do you have an older car?"

"Yes, and her name is Sara," he said, grinning.

"You named your car?"

"Not usually, but this old car asked me to name her Sara. So, when your car asks, you gotta listen."

She stared at him with curiosity and an ounce of caution. *Hmm, this guy is strange.*

Suddenly realizing his sarcasm, it hit her, and she laughed. "I'm sorry, I, you see, I sort of thought you were serious. I'm not very sharp today." Now, really embarrassed, she quickly changed the subject. "How long have you worked here?"

That's a good question, don't make a fool of yourself. Keep him talking. Virginia's nerves began to settle.

"I've been here a few years now. I like it, and it's close to home. I live in Redlands. Just me and my golden retriever. She's just a puppy."

"I like Redlands. I love old homes. My brother-in-law's family, the Smiths, grew up in one of the oldest houses in town. It's on Olive Street, and it's surrounded by orange groves." *Doing good, Virginia.*

"I know the house. It's set back in the orange groves. I also live in an old home. It's a corner lot. Do you live in Redlands?"

"No, I don't." With a sudden urge to end the conversation before it got too personal, she said, "Well, nice talking to you. I am taking a short lunch. Lots to do." *You're lying, Virginia. You don't have lots to do.*

Charlie stood. "Oh, of course. Well, thanks for letting me join you."

Before Virginia walked away, he said with a warm smile, "If you ever need help with your old car, you know…repairs, I offer my services. I love working on them."

She thanked him with a nod and hurried back to the library.

She darted into the restroom, examined her face and teeth, and to her relief, there was no food. "Good grief, what are you so worried about? He is just a co-worker who happens to be a man."

She stepped out, returned to her desk, and sat, staring out the window. Again, strange thoughts of not being divorced swirled, and her lunch began to sour. She let out a sigh of frustration as she gloomily went back to her duties.

The day ended, and Virginia made her way to her car. Sitting in it, she turned the key, and it clicked. *Oh no.* Turning it again, it only clicked some more, then nothing. She leaned her head back, stared up at the car roof, and muttered, "Great…just great."

She stepped out and approached the large hood. Clicking the latch, she lifted the hunk of iron and figured it was an excellent place to start. Staring at the motor, she thought, *What on earth is all this stuff?* It looked like dirty, oily pieces of metal. *I have no idea what this junk is besides a motor. What did my brother tell me to look for again?*

"Need some help?"

Virginia leaped and nearly hit her head on the hood.

There was Charlie, only this time, not smiling but looking remorseful. "My gosh, I am something else, aren't I?"

"You're three for three!" Virginia said. "But I will take you up on your offer. It won't start. It just clicks, and then nothing."

"Hmm, let me look at your battery. It's always the first place to start." He dove under and began checking the terminals.

"That's what my brother told me I was supposed to look for," Virginia said, remembering. "Always start with the battery. Well, at least I opened the hood," She mused.

"Yep, it looks like this may be the problem. Hop in and turn the key. I'm going to try and tighten the terminal; it's loose."

She turned the key, and it started.

With a grin, Charlie popped his head from under the hood and motioned for Virginia to shut the engine off. "Let me get my wrench. I'll be right back."

Virginia eyed him as he walked away, and quickly, she adjusted her rear-view mirror. Checking her hair and lips, to her surprise, all was in order.

Charlie returned and promptly made the repair and said, "Your battery is old and corroded, and the terminal is nearly cracked off. I can change it if you like. My treat."

"You can do that?" *You can do that? Of course, he can, you idiot. What kind of question was that?*

She wrestled with her thoughts. "I mean, are you offering to pay for the battery? How much are they?"

Wiping his hands and moving closer, he said, "They are a little over twenty bucks, and I'll help if you'll let me?"

Don't let him…don't let him. "I tell you what, I will buy it, and you install it. How is that?"

"It's a deal. It's Friday, do you want me to come over? Or do you want to do it now? What would you like, Virginia?"

I don't have twenty dollars to my name. What were you thinking? Good grief. "I will have to wait for the next payday. Then we can." *Great, now he knows how poor you are.*

"I tell you what, I will pick one up, come by your house tomorrow, and you can pay me whenever you like."

Taken aback by this offer, Virginia thought, *This man is really nice. I can't commit to anything but just friends. I don't know what he's looking for other than just being kind to me. I can't date, I can't even think of another man in my life, nor do I want to.*

Eventually, she gave in. "Sure, let me write down my address. Maybe around lunch, that's the least I can do?" she said, handing him the paper.

She sat down, started the car, and pulled away. She felt something like guilt rise in her. Immediately she regretted everything that had just happened.

Virginia couldn't sleep a wink that night. Was it nerves? Regret? Or maybe something else? She rolled over in bed and saw the time.

When she got up, Virginia pondered a way to tell the kids. She made pancakes and bacon, and the troops were seated.

Once seated, she said, "Kids, a nice man is coming over around lunch. His name is Charlie. He is going to fix the car. I want you to…"

The kids all stared, and some giggled.

"You got a date, Mom?" Patrick laughed, and Maureen looked shocked and worried that a strange man was coming over.

"Now, kids, don't be rude and interrupt. Charlie worked on the car yesterday because it wouldn't start. The battery is old and needs a new one, and his help will give my sister a break. I'm always asking her and Andy for favors. Besides, he will be surprised when he sees how many children I have, like in the old Mother Goose story. At least we have a home, and I am not the old lady who lives in a shoe," she mused.

"Hey, you mean to feed us broth, then whip us and send us to bed?" Cynthia shouted, and all stared. "Well, that's how the nursery rhyme goes with the lady in the shoe. She feeds her kids broth, whips them, and sends them to bed."

"Hmm, not a bad idea once in a while. Easy to make a cauldron of broth." Virginia stood, laughing to herself, as she began cleaning the kitchen.

Keith looked at Paul nervously because they both had been spanked before bed more than once.

Paul thought maybe there was truth to the old story. *Could our mom really be the old lady?*

Keith shrugged and thought back to Charlie. "Mom, what kind of car does he have?"

"I don't know. He drives a truck. He did mention he has a really old car. Maybe he will drive it. I don't know. But one thing I do know," she said sternly, staring at the boys, "you will not climb all over his car or get inside without permission, is that clear?"

"Loud and clear, Mom!" Patrick shouted as if in the military, followed by a salute, and the boys sped out to wait for Charlie.

Maureen hesitantly remained behind, silent and staring. Virginia passed her into the kitchen and stopped. "Now, Maureen, don't worry. I have no plans of dating anyone. He's just an acquaintance from work who happens to be a man. Stop worrying. It's written all over your face."

"I'm sorry…it just seems strange."

Maureen excused herself to her room, and Virginia sighed as she watched her go. She knew her concerns and why Maureen had always been wary.

Virginia thought back to years earlier. There was a Father-Daughter event when Maureen was in Brownies, the beginning years of Girl Scouts. Maureen had been so excited about it; her heart was set on the idea that her real father would come to be with her.

"Maureen, please, he is not coming. He doesn't even know this event exist. So don't think he will be there," Virginia consoled.

"But I know he will," Maureen insisted.

But as a young girl, it was impossible not to get your hopes up. Maureen pleaded to attend the event. So, Virginia let her. Knowing full well it was going to be a tough lesson.

And finally, at the father-daughter affair, she waited and waited, hopelessly watching the door. As the evening passed, her dreams slowly faded when she realized that her father would never come. She was the only girl there without a father by her side. It crushed her.

Being young and abandoned by someone you thought loved you, someone you thought could never let you down, never stopped hurting for many years. Maureen was the oldest, and this trauma affected her the most because she remembered her father, and a few kids only had vague memories. Now, after hearing another man was coming over, she was uncomfortable.

Virginia, seeing the sorrow in Maureen's eyes, walked over to her closed bedroom door. She reached for the handle but then stopped. She remembered when she was Maureen's age and how much she missed her father while the navy had him deployed out to sea. Then when Virginia turned sixteen, he died from a heart attack. It was hard enough then. Knowing that Maureen felt abandoned, she began to worry. *So many times, I'm in survivor mode. I guess I don't take enough time to learn how my kids are feeling. Chalk it up to another thing the single parent has to remember. Lord God…help me help my children.*

Before she knew it, it was lunchtime, and Maureen surfaced to help, showing the real nature of her heart. And right on cue, an old beige car barreled up the long driveway. Of course, the four boys ran up the drive escorting the visitor up the driveway barefooted with cut-off shorts. *Like a pack of wolves,* Virginia thought. *Well, the cat's out of the bag. He now knows that I'm divorced, and I have a ton of children, and they look like they are from the backwoods. Virginia, you could have cleaned them up!*

While Virginia checked the mirror again, Cynthia noticed Mom looked unusually nicer for a Saturday. "Mom, you look pretty," she commented.

Virginia paused as a sudden embarrassment wrenched her face. Now flustered, she took a deep breath and stepped outside; the girls looked at each other with raised eyebrows.

Maureen sighed and asked, "Well, you want to go meet him?"

Cynthia nodded as they stared out the front window.

"Then let's get this over with."

Cynthia looked at Charlie and said, "He looks nice."

Soon, Charlie counted six children and stared at Virginia with a sort of, *Wow, what a strong woman.* Yet, he showed great compassion.

"Well, now, I'm Charlie, and what are your names?"

One by one, the bouncing boys shouted their names, and he shook their hands. Their excitement turned ten notches as they circled the old car with fascination.

Charlie then turned to the girls, humbly approached them, and introduced himself like a true gentleman. His gentleness diffused the girls' restraint, mostly Maureen's, and they felt that, indeed, he was a nice man.

"Hello Virginia, you have a wonderful family." Charlie shook her hand as well.

"Well, now you know why I have no money until payday." *Really Virginia, really, that's all you can say. What a blunder!*

Chuckling at this, Charlie said, "Like I said, you can pay whenever or not at all. I'm in no hurry. Now, what men want to help me fix their mother's car?"

All boys' hands were raised, still bouncing.

"Alright then, let's get a move on, and then maybe, afterward, if you do a good job, I will introduce you to Sara."

The boys stared at Charlie as Greg blurted, "Who's Sara?"

They were wondering if a girl was maybe hiding in the car.

"Sara is my talking car." He pointed to the old 1947 Ford and asked for a wrench from his toolbox.

Patrick was in charge of the tools, Greg held the rag, and Keith and Paul were too short to see what was going on under the hood.

Keith grabbed their grandpa's old bucket and flipped it over as both he and Paul teetered and watched, acting as if they were helping. Thoughts of a talking car fascinated them.

Paul stared at the automobile, wondering if the bumper was the mouth and headlights the eyes.

Soon the old was out, and the new battery was in, and Charlie handed the keys to Patrick and said, "Start her up!"

Patrick looked proud that this responsibility was given to him. He strutted to the seat and wondered, *Where do I put the key?*

Fudging with the key, he shoved it in and turned, and the car quickly started. Charlie gave the thumbs up and motioned to shut it down.

Virginia came to the door and smiled.

Patrick was beaming along with the helpers.

Virginia stared at the boys, seeing their excitement when a man was with them, showing them how to work with tools. She felt a small sense of relief. "Lunch is ready!" she announced, but the boys were too distracted by the possibility of a real talking car.

"But Mom!" Patrick yelled.

"No buts!" Virginia responded.

They all washed and sat around the table, eager for new stories from Charlie.

Sandwiches were stacked, fresh fruit was cut, and a large bowl of potato chips lured them. After the pouring of never-ending powdered lemonade, they said grace. The kids felt embarrassed, but their mom always insisted. In the end, Charlie loudly said, "Amen!"

The kids giggled and listened to Charlie and their mom sharing boring work stuff, which made them all quickly lose interest.

"Charlie?" Keith spoke. "Do you like my mommy?"

"Keith!" Virginia stared, eyes wide and blushing.

For the first time, they couldn't get a read on her face. Her expression was a mixture of slightly angry, surprised, happy, and mortified. Waves of snickers and laughter circled the table, yet Maureen showed no response but worry.

"Why yes, Keith, I do. Your mom and I work together, and she is my nice friend. Just like all of you. I like each one of you, and boys, you are good mechanics, and girls, this is the best and most fun lunch I ever had." Charlie took another bite.

"When can we see your far-out, talking car?" Patrick asked eagerly, ready to bolt outside at any moment.

"What? He has a talking car?" Cynthia looked outside, staring at the old car. "How does it talk?"

"Well, if it's alright with your mother, and you are all finished with lunch, I will introduce you to Sara."

"Sara, your car is a girl?" Cynthia was still staring outside with wonder. "It looks like a boy. Not a girl."

With much laughter, Virginia nodded, and the gang sped to the front door. Before they escaped, their mom yelled, "Mind your manners, and do not touch that car unless you have permission!"

Smiling at Charlie, she turned and joined Maureen in the kitchen.

Maureen stayed behind, secretly curious about wanting to see a talking car. Acting grown-up, her choice was to be in her mom's company. Still, on every trip to clear the table, her eyes were drawn to the automobile's mysterious secrets.

~

"Kids, this is a 1947 Mercury. Treat her gently. Now, Patrick, you open the door, and I'll open mine. I need you to all squeeze in. Sara would like that. She loves showing off!"

Charlie inserted the key into the ignition and started her. The motor purred, and the kid's excitement was at an all-time high.

Paul stared with great anticipation. Keith was mesmerized by the old knobs and dials. Patrick and Greg strained to see out the front window while Cynthia stared at Charlie, suspicious of the whole affair.

"Would you all like to hear music?" Many shouts of "Yes," arose.

"Sara, the kids would like to hear music…turn on Sara."

To everyone's surprise, the old dash radio instantly lit up with blaring big band orchestra music. Cynthia stared at Charlie because he didn't even move a muscle. The kids were ecstatic, looking at Charlie and staring at the radio.

"Far out!" Greg shouted.

Patrick quickly began commanding the car. "Turn off Sara, drive Sara, honk the horn, Sara! Hey, it's not working for me!"

"Because Sara does not like to be yelled at or bossed around, she likes a gentle voice, one that shows respect. Cynthia, ask Sara kindly to turn the radio off."

Charlie held up his hands in plain view.

A slew of commands shouted from all the kids except Cynthia, all wanting to be first to control the car. But Charlie shook his head in disappointment. "Ah, ah, ah, she does not like that. What's that, Sara, only one more command you will listen to?" He paused. "Okay, I am sorry, kids. She now will only listen to Cynthia. Go ahead."

Proudly and kindly, Cynthia quietly said, "Sara, please turn off your radio?" And sure enough, the radio instantly turned off, to everyone's amazement."

Smiles abounded, and flashes of Chitty-Chitty-Bang-Bang filled everyone's minds.

Charlie turned the car off, and the kids piled out in wonder, then sprinted to the house to be the first to tell the tale to their mother. Of course, Patrick was the fastest.

As they circled Mom, Patrick nudged Greg and pulled him aside. Slowly sneaking away, they slinked to the backyard.

Patrick said, "Listen, it's worth getting in trouble. I gotta know how he does it. Let's sneak into the car and find out its secret."

"It'll be far out if we can. Wait, so the car really only talks through the radio? I thought it would really talk, like with a voice. Saying cool things like, far-out!" Greg joked.

"I don't care. I want to know how he does it. Let's split!"

While the rest were enjoying ice cream in the house, the spies slithered to the driver's door and slowly began to open it.

Giggling, Patrick said, "Barely hold the door open. This has to be fast."

Quickly scanning, there was nothing obvious; Patrick said, "There has to be a secret button somewhere." He speedily examined the dash and then the floor; the door swung wide.

The boys jumped!

Charlie was staring them down. "Sara does not like it when people sneak in without permission."

The boys, frozen, suddenly weighed their thoughts of the mission versus the wrath they were about to receive from Mom. Gulping hard, they quickly apologized.

"Now, do you boys want some ice cream?"

"Yes, sir," they said as one.

Slowly walking into the house and through the front door came Charlie, Patrick, and Greg.

Virginia glared. "Where did you run off to? You are going to miss ice cream. Is that what you want?"

Their mother began scooping ice cream into their bowls. With heads down, prepared for punishment, they readied for the wrath to come.

But to their surprise, Charlie said, "They must not have heard we had ice cream, so I went and told them before we eat it all."

Looking down at them, he slyly winked. The boys stared at him and then at each other. Their dessert awaited them, so they smiled and ran for their treat. From that day on, Patrick and Greg held Charlie in the highest regard.

Charlie had brought a different friendship to the home. That Saturday, having a man visiting had been truly fun.

It was impossible to be left alone when Virginia walked him to the car, which was somewhat preferred. The children provided a barrier, and Virginia wasn't keen on tapping into feelings that went outside the bonds of friendship.

Charlie waved to the kids, and some shook his hand.

"Thank you, Charlie, really, this was a huge help, and we are all very thankful. As soon as I can get ahead, I will pay you for the battery," she said, wondering where and when she could scrape up additional cash, which seemed a million years away.

"Nope, you don't need to, Virginia. The delicious lunch, dessert, and, most of all, meeting your wonderful and well-mannered children was worth so much. I should owe you money," he joked. "Truly, you are a strong and wonderful woman."

With that, he started the old car with a loud command, "Turn on Sara!"

The radio blared, and he waved as he drove down the long driveway. And, as was the custom, the escort of boys and Cynthia ran along the car, seeing him off.

Chapter 11

Lockheed Layoffs

During this long year of 1972, being able to drive herself to Mentone for work changed Virginia's world. Endless stops at the grocery store helped more than anyone knew.

At this time, Virginia enrolled in night school. She needed to be fluent in shorthand to get a better job down the road. Leaving Maureen in charge of watching her siblings, Virginia was on a mission to better herself.

A small bonus was that she found some peace and quiet by being able to finish her studies at school. Once in a while, she would hire a sitter when funds were available. But she trusted Maureen's ability to run the troops in their proper directions. Virginia knew it was a tiresome task, but she quickly learned a timely and important one.

In the few months that followed, Charlie's visits had become more frequent. The kids were excited every time he showed up. His handyman skills and knowledge of automobiles kept Virginia above water with many needed repairs. Their friendship slowly grew, and her trust in him flourished.

One morning while parking her jalopy at work, Mary was a few cars away. Her nasal voice rang out. "Not riding the bus anymore, I see. Did you finally get yourself a car? Good thing you don't owe money on that old beater. There's nothing but bad rumors floating around. It sounds like we're all going to lose our jobs."

As Mary stormed away, Virginia's heart thumped. Walking into the building, she noticed the mood seemed downcast. She didn't want to believe the gossip but couldn't help but wonder if it was true. *I just got this job…I can't afford to be laid off. God, please, no.*

The atmosphere in the breakroom was quite different than usual. The traditional chit-chat was absent from the area, and high-heeled shoes clicking about were also absent. It was strange to only hear typewriters in the distance.

The walk to the library was also surprisingly quiet. This day was dark. A cloud of misery shrouded the entire place.

After a few worrisome hours, Virginia checked the clock. It was almost break time. Soon the time arrived, and she quickly hurried to the breakroom and poured a cup of coffee. She listened intently to the gossip. After approaching her fellow employees, gathered around the tables, she overheard several conversations about a new space program and many uncertainties.

Then a familiar voice spoke up in conversation. It was Charlie asking for more details.

One man answered, "Yes, the new shuttle projects are starting at full swing and are top secret, so they want to downsize to keep it under wraps. Most likely, all of the new people will lose their jobs."

Charlie added, "No, not just us newer people. It's all of us. This is Lockheed's great opportunity to scale down, even those of you who have been here for years."

One man, furious, jumped to his feet and yelled, "We have our heads on the chopping block? No one is safe…and yes, it sucks!" The man took a long drag of his cigarette and walked away.

"Mary?" Virginia approached her. "Is this true? I mean, this is not just gossip?"

"Sorry, Virginia, we think it is. You know what I think? The bigwigs making the decisions that punish our lives can stick it up their noses!" Mary vented.

"Darn it, woman, tell us how you really feel!" A group of men laughed at Mary as they headed in when the bell sounded.

Virginia, very quiet, felt a lump rising in her throat. Now was not the time to cry. Holding back tears, she returned to her duties. She focused only on her work and prayed silently as she did so.

Charlie walked in and could tell she was upset. "Hello Virginia, I was just checking in to see how you were doing."

"Hey Charlie, I don't know if I can talk now," she said grimly while looking out the window. "You're the only one who knows my situation. I can't lose my job. I haven't even paid you yet for the battery a few months ago. Or the used tire and the extra fuel. All the times you have taken the kids for rides and bought them ice cream."

"You don't owe me for any of that. That was all free," Charlie said, smiling gently at her. "Well, we'll hope for the best, and if there is anything I can do to help, please, Virginia, let me know." Slowly he turned and walked toward the door.

"Charlie?" she said, turning away from the window. "Thank you, really. Thanks for all you have done for the kids and for me. They really like you."

"What about you…do you really like me?" he asked, staring.

Virginia looked down and smiled slightly. It seemed to last forever.

The large door swung wide open about each other's feelings, and burning erupted in her heart. *Virginia, you fool, stop saying things like this. You're only making it worse. You're still married, and you've got to stop this!*

Mustering up all her courage, she looked up and stated, "Like I said, we all really like you."

A long pause floated in the air, and then Charlie nodded and stepped out the door.

Virginia swung around and clenched her fist. *I can't do this!*

Screaming on the inside she felt torn between her Catholic beliefs and her feelings for Charlie. A rage began to rise within her; its ignition point stemmed from shattered dreams and broken promises.

The slamming books and shoving carts commenced until the noise levels loudly echoed throughout the lonely building, and her heart melted. Virginia stopped and stared around the library. The rows of books seemed to mock her loneliness, like her old piano at home. *I feel like I have knowledge, creativity, music, stories, and good memories, but I'm growing old alone on the shelf of single motherhood. Every day is a struggle for me, a challenge. I can't even get my head above financial woes and the ugly stress of it. I'm too scared to share my life with Charlie. I will die alone, and no one will ever understand who I really am.*

Her thoughts pierced her soul as a tidal wave of sadness drowned her in heavy sobs.

Running to the restroom, she slammed the door and screamed, "I'm not even divorced! I'm bound in a one-sided contract! Does it ever end? Can it get any worse?"

Virginia stayed there for a moment with her head in her hands, feeling the weight of her life on her shoulders. *I just...want to be happy.*

A thought hit her suddenly that maybe she would never truly be happy. There was always a new burden weighing her down, one thing after another. She knew the only time she was ever truly happy was when she thought of her children.

Each of their six faces popped up in her mind, and a sense of peace began to come over her. She took a deep breath and collected herself. *I hope no one walked in and heard my meltdown; that would be a first.*

She fixed her makeup, slowly opened the door, and all was quiet.

The lunch bell rang, and she locked the world out of the library. "Charlie is the only one I've ever met who seems to generally care...and he's so good with the kids. But, God, I am...I'm," she wiped a tear. "God in Heaven, I hurt deep down. All I feel is fear of lonely pain."

After lunch, her boss called her and asked her to come to his office right away. With a shaky hand, she set the phone down.

Before she left, she looked out the window at the swaying trees and the blue sky. She wondered in an instant what Maureen, Patrick, Greg, Cynthia, Keith, and Pauly, were up to. What were they thinking? How will losing her job affect them, let alone her insides? *God, please be with me.*

After letting out a long breath, a lump caught in her throat. Her stomach felt queasy, and she was thankful she hadn't eaten her lunch.

Her gut seemed to tell her what it was about. So, with tension in every step toward her boss's office, she prepared herself to take the news.

She knocked, then opened the door slowly and was invited to sit.

The unwelcome news that her job was ending came as no surprise to her.

"You can work the next few months. Then the changes will take place. Sorry, Virginia, you're a great worker," her boss added, twiddling his thumbs as he looked at her sympathetically.

The news caused twisted knots in her stomach. She expected to lose her job, yes, but it was still hard to take.

She chose her next words carefully. "Is there anything else I could do? I haven't been working here long, and," she steadied herself, "I need my job. I will take a cut in pay, please?"

"Everyone else laid off needs their job as well. You are not alone. Now, I think it's reasonable that you can stay on for two more months, but then, that's it."

Frustration grew, and Virginia didn't want to play the helpless mother of six, card, but the words seemed to slip out, "I'm a single mother with six children! I'm struggling through night school to gain the skills to better my job. Please, my work here is pretty close to home! I have been riding buses to get here every day. And by God's good graces, I have managed to feed my kids and get them off to school. And now, now..." Halting her words, she shamefully stood. Her outburst brought embarrassment. "I'm so sorry. Please forgive my outburst. It's not your fault. Thank you for letting me stay on. I'm incredibly grateful."

Turning, she headed for the door for a quick exit.

Her boss shouted after her. "Virginia, I, look, I had no idea. In fact, I have never heard of such a thing. Six children? Are you making this up?"

Slowly moving her head from left to right, letting the motion answer, *no, I am not making this up.*

"Good gracious, Virginia," he said with a shocked look on his face. "Look, there's a company I know of that's hiring. They're over in Banning. I do have a friend there, and he said they're looking to hire a few positions. Here, let me give you his name and their address, and phone number. I know it's further away, but maybe it's a lead." He scribbled the information, and he handed her the paper.

She nodded and squeaked out a thank you as he said, "Good luck!"

Stepping out the door, she felt like a total failure. Her emotions ran high as she repeated under her breath, "Good luck, good luck? I bust my butt to get on my feet, and all he can say is good luck? It wasn't luck that carried me this far." She scoffed.

She headed for the library, entered, and sat behind her desk. Again, an unsettling knot twisted in her gut as waves of fear ignited. She looked around quickly to make sure she was alone before she thundered out, "Breathe, Virginia. Calm down. Just calm down." She added with a sarcastic tone, "So, you don't have a job; you're in really great shape."

The day drew to quitting time as she wrapped up the last of her tasks. She stood at the window and stared out at the mountains. Thinking hard about certain events in life and their impeccable timing. She had reminder thoughts of her six children, her two moves already, and the number of people who came to her aid.

She sighed and prayed aloud. "God, now I know why you gave me this car. It's perfect timing for me to be able to drive and look for a new job. But, if it's going to be in Banning, do we have to move again? Re-plant the kids in new schools?" She shook her head and said, "I already feel an ulcer coming on. And the stress, the stress…" Pacing and looking out the window, she said, "Forgive me for my several outburst and pity party earlier, I guess I am feeling sorry for myself, and I don't need to be so selfish. I can do this with Your help."

"Are you talking to yourself, Virginia?" Mary said as she entered. "Well, did you receive the news yet? Sorry if you did. I know you haven't worked here long. But that is how it goes sometimes. You just have to keep fighting. As for me, well, I don't need my job. I just work because I'm bored, but I guess others aren't as fortunate as me. Anyway, dear, I'm returning my boss's books on engineering that have been on my desk for months." She set them in the return bin, turned, and headed for the exit. "See you around."

The door closed, and she was gone.

"Me? I'm fine, thanks for asking?" Virginia mockingly said. "What a selfish woman," she said as she emptied the bin and placed the books back in their place.

Grabbing her things, she clocked out and headed for her car. The lot was full of beautiful and new autos. And there, in the middle of luxury, was her beat-up and faded white Chevy with a glistening duct-tape interior.

A few would glance her way and then at her car, then back at her, with a questionable look in their eyes. To quickly escape and avoid Charlie, she drove away. Her stomach still burned the whole ride home.

Oblivious to the route or if the sun was shining or not, she suddenly was pulling into her home. Virginia stopped by the mailbox. She stared down the long drive and wondered if their days were numbered at her mother's house. *How will I tell the kids? Maybe I can get another closer job.*

Entering her home, she was greeted by the mob. Hugs and kisses abounded, followed by the usual questions about work, when and what's for dinner, and whether she had fun driving her car.

After sufficient answers, Virginia changed into her comfortable slacks and a sweatshirt and started in the kitchen. Pulling together ingredients to spruce up the spam, beans, and powdered potatoes, she began mixing and slicing. Occasionally she would look out to the backyard as one or two of the boys sped by.

Maureen was occupied with homework next to Cynthia. Both had books open, and Virginia noticed the older boys' books looked untouched.

Paul came in and hugged her leg, then stared up at her.

"What do you want, Pauly?" she asked, ruffling his hair.

Round-eyed and grinning, he said, "I love you, Mommy."

"Oh, bless your heart," she said, setting down her cooking spoon.

She knelt, eye level with her baby, and asked, "Can you help me with dinner? I need the table set and cleared."

"Yep," he said, hopping over to help move books along with his sisters.

Keith, too, pitched in, and soon, all sat for dinner. The mood was quiet, and Maureen kept a close eye on her mother, who was noticeably silent.

"Mom, is everything alright?" she asked.

Even at twelve, Maureen always had a sense of when things weren't all right, and Virginia knew she couldn't hide it.

Frustrated, she stated, "No, things are not alright."

She set her fork down and looked at all of them. "I'm losing my job, and I don't know what to do, and the last thing we need is to move again. I mean, Banning! What's in Banning besides the beginning of the dry desert?" Her voice began to elevate. "Why can't we just stay put? I'm sick and tired of things never working out. It's miserable always having to worry about how to feed my family and keep you kids clothed. Gosh, I wish…"— she exhaled—"I wish we could just catch a break! We get a car, and now I lose my job. Good grief!"

Reaching for another bite, she chewed fast.

Silence ruled the six pairs of eyes fixed on her face. It was quiet as they were stunned by the news.

Patrick, who always looked at change as a new adventure, broke the silence. "We have to move? Cool! Where are we moving to? Will there be places to hike? Where is Banning? Isn't that in the desert?"

Greg stood. "We're moving to the desert? That's cool!"

Cynthia giggled. "Are there cactus? Won't we get poked by them? I heard they hurt. Can we get a cat in our new home?"

Keith retorted, "No! I want a dog?"

Virginia smiled and shook her head. "You kids see the fun in everything, don't you?" Leaning back, she said, "What would I do without you? Maureen, don't worry. Sorry for my outburst, but sometimes…it just comes out."

Paul walked over to Mom and hugged her again. "I'll help us move."

Soon, all volunteered as talk of moving seemed to ignite the bunch.

Virginia settled and listened to their excitement, overhearing them repeat that, indeed, this house was exceedingly small but had a huge yard. *Maybe, just maybe, there is something we could afford and finally give grandma back her home. But first, I need to find a job.*

The next evening after dinner, the phone rang, and to her surprise, it was her mother. "Hello Virginia, how are you and the kids?"

"Oh, we're fine. How are you doing, Mom?" she asked as Maureen and Cynthia huddled around.

"Well, for an old lady, I'm getting along nicely. I'm calling because of my retirement. It's official, and I will be leaving Alabama and heading for Yucaipa. I found an apartment already, up the street, on the boulevard, below Flag Hill Park. If it all goes well, I will be home in one week. But don't worry, you can still have the house as long as you need it. I can't wait to see my grandkids. Have they grown?"

"Yes, they have. We can't wait to see you too. Everything here is going well, and I guess we will see you in a week."

"Is all else good? How is your job working out?"

Nervously looking down at the girls, she said, "It's a job, and it pays the bills...well, some of the bills. I'll tell you all of the news when you arrive. I have baths to draw and clean up before bed. We love you, Mom, and will see you shortly."

Virginia rushed off the phone and said goodbye. Looking at her daughters, awaiting answers, she said, "Look, your grandma has a lot to think about and doesn't need to know yet. I will tell her when she settles in."

Cynthia looked confused. "But aren't you lying?"

"No, because I still have my job for a spell. That's the silver lining in the clouds...meaning, there's still good news to our crazy life."

Chapter 12

What to Do?

After a long week of worry, it turned to thoughtful prayer. Virginia gazed at the phone number her boss gave for a possible job lead during her lunch break. Fidgety, she picked up the phone and dialed. With only a few words exchanged, the company quickly requested an interview the following week.

Nerves were already beginning to set in. The time seemed to rocket by, and the weekend was a blur. Before Virginia knew it, she was heading to Banning for her interview with an unsettled heart.

As she turned south off the freeway, she faced the Idyllwild mountains and was captured by the view. The mountains seemed to tempt her to keep driving up the steep road to escape her worries. However, the fantasy vanished as she turned left, and the Deutsch Company's large buildings came into view.

The buildings spread over several acres, and Virginia was impressed. The company's enormity suddenly made her feel quite small and very unqualified. Immediately, she began doubting her abilities if maybe this was a massive waste of time. Instant stomach worries ignited.

She approached the guard gate, curious how she would pass through the fortress, but she saw the guard waving her toward him.

"Hello, I am here for an interview," she said with a quiver in her voice.

The friendly guard said, "Yes, ma'am, you are to go straight and follow the visitor signs."

His smile eased her tensions a bit now, knowing she was expected.

Virginia parked the old car and walked into the office. A kind lady directed her where to go. She made her way into the waiting room and sat down slowly. A quick scan showed that several interviews were being conducted. Staring at the other ladies ahead of her, she noticed that their dresses were new, their youth showed, and some wore lovely jewelry, the likes she didn't even know existed. Raising six children kept her out of the loop of cultural fashion.

Setting her large purse to cover the hole in her coat, next to the small oil stain from adding it to her old Chevy, she shyly looked out the window with another bout of unwelcome waves of doubt. While staring out the window into the towering mountain ranges, she was rather impressed with the pass area. She had driven through it but never stopped long enough to notice its beauty. *Well, Virginia,* she thought, *it's a long shot.*

Thirty minutes passed, and the line of ladies came and went, with their stylish clothes and beautiful hair, until her name was called. *God, please help me. I don't think I stand a chance.*

Stepping into the office, the pleasant gentleman introduced himself, and his secretary sat to his right.

"You are Virginia and are currently employed with Lockheed? Sad to hear about their layoffs. So, we are looking to hire a few secretaries, and of course, there are more applicants than we have available positions. Tell us about yourself."

Sitting back in his chair, he folded his hands together. He stared motionless at Virginia as they waited for her response.

Sit up straight, Virginia, don't choke. "Thank you for this opportunity, and yes, I am being laid off. My boss said I am a good worker and that I kept their research library in excellent shape."

Her hands started sweating, and a wave of heat began to overtake her as she realized she did not remove her coat and that the office was warm. With beads of sweat running down her back, her stomach began to ache as she was flustered with thinking of a polite way to remove her coat while trying not to act nervous.

"Hold it, librarian? We are looking for skilled secretaries that can record minutes, type fast, file, and mail documents in a speedy manner. Librarian experience, I don't think fits what we are looking for, do you?"

Act confident, Virginia. You have mouths to feed. Slowly stand, remove your coat, and look like you are getting down to business.

Politely, she said, "If you will excuse me." She stood, nicely approached the coat rack, hung it slowly, and sat back down. Clearing her throat, out came, "Being a librarian or secretary are one and the same. They both involve filing, organizing, tracking, and typing. I am trained with the latest IBMs and can type over sixty words a minute. If that isn't enough, I will use shorthand to write minutes for all meetings, so nothing will be missed in any conversation. I started learning when I worked at the Long Beach Shipyards years ago, and I am still quite good at it. If that is not enough, I am a single mom with six children, so I will be faithful and do all I can to be here on time because I need to work and feed my family. I will be a loyal employee for years to come if you see fit to hire me."

The man sat forward and exchanged a glance with his secretary. They were both wide-eyed.

Staring back, he said, "Six children, a single mom? Wow, you must know hard work. How do you get any rest? My wife and I can't keep up with our two children, let alone six?" Motioning to his secretary, he said, "Can you get Virginia a pen and notepad, please?"

Handing her the pad, the man said, "Okay, I would like to dictate, and you write what I say in shorthand. Ready, go."

He began a lengthy conversation about the company's language, consisting of foreign words for connectors, wires, shipments, and jet airliner accounts.

After several minutes, he ended and pointed to his secretary, who began to speak for another two minutes. Finally, he waved her to stop. "Well, how did you do?"

Virginia read back the entire conversation, and as she concluded, it was clear she didn't miss one word. The two were quiet as she paused, then suddenly continued reading, in shorthand, her answer to his earlier question when he asked, how do you get any rest?

She wrote in shorthand, *If you must know, my rest is sufficient, and yes, having six children is hard work, but I love my children and wouldn't trade this life for anything. This tough life has taught me how to use these skills everywhere I go.*

Doubtful, the man asked, "Wait a minute, you really answered my question as well?" Pointing to his secretary, she approached and asked for the notepad.

His secretary read quietly with eyebrows raised, then said, "Wow, she even recorded everything you said about your wife and how you can't keep up with your two children. Very impressive."

"Virginia, you live in Yucaipa?" the man asked.

"Yes, but that is no worry. If I am considered for the job, we will move if we have to."

"That's why I ask. My friend is a realtor, and they are selling, well, these HUD homes in Banning for people in your situation. They are four-bedroom homes. No landscaping, of course, but they're available. In fact, a few of them have been sitting for a long time. And since we would like to hire you, it's an option."

"Well, thank you very much, but I can't afford a home, and besides, I really need to find employment before I would even dream of making such a commitment, but thanks."

Virginia stood as the words played back in her mind, "Did…you say you wanted to hire me?"

"Yes, we have interviewed several applicants, but none have the skill in shorthand, and that sets you above the rest. Are you interested?" The man stood.

Flushed, she smiled. "Yes, very, thank you, thank you. I will. Maybe I can…When do you want me to start?"

"You can give your notice and then come aboard. I will let Jay, your new boss, know he can expect you in a few weeks."

He then gave her the number of his realtor friend. They shook hands, and she left the office.

Virginia returned to her car. She motored her way to the exit but quickly pulled over. Tears formed as she sat beaming, replaying what had just happened. *Thank you, God, thank you.*

Thankfulness bled from her heart as a huge burden felt lifted. *A job, a secretary's job. I'm a secretary now. You did it, Virginia!*

Checking her watch, Virginia realized she still had several hours before she had to return home. She headed to a local service station and found a payphone. She dropped her dime in the slot and dialed the number of the realtor. The realtor gave her directions to the few homes for sale that she could look at.

Virginia followed Ramsey Street, then turned on the obscure dirt road called Omar. When she turned, she noticed a red antique store. She wondered if she could afford what was displayed in the windows.

Barreling up West Jacinto View Road, she found 40th street and became giddy. The neighborhood was quiet, and she noticed several vacant lots and a few mature homes filled the rest. Finding the correct address, she pulled in front of the house. The weeds stood taller than her youngest boys, and there was a lone, four-foot-high palm tree out front near the driveway.

What a cute little palm, she thought.

Excited, she felt an attractive quietness rule the neighborhood. She walked to the front porch, cupped her hands, and peered inside. "This must be the dining room. Wow, it's more open and roomier."

Her heart leaped when she saw the spacious kitchen.

She sighed. "There is no way I can afford this. Keep dreaming, Virginia."

A car arrived, and out came two realtors. They unlocked the house, and to her surprise, there were four bedrooms and two baths down the long hall. *Two bathrooms? What a luxury.*

The home was as plain as could be. The restrooms had no cabinets because the lavatories were wall-hung with exposed plumbing. There were fiberglass tubs and showers and a two-car garage.

Surrounded by foothills and large empty fields, she felt for sure there was more room here for her kids to roam than in Yucaipa. The yard was small, but the neighborhood was far from any busy highway, and only ten houses were on the street. When she stepped outside, she hadn't noticed before, but the view of the mountains was incredible.

"I love the view of the mountains," she said in wonder.

"It's a nice property, and we have reduced the price since it's been sitting for a while, as you can probably tell by the size of the weeds. There are also loans you may qualify for, some for the well-to-do and one for low-income families. Think about it, will you?"

"I'm definitely low income. I doubt I would qualify for any of the loans. Although, it's fun to look at. Thank you for your time." She nodded and headed for her car.

One of the realtors chased after her. "Please, take our card, give us a call. Really, you would be surprised about the low-income loan. It's based on your salary. So, the payments won't be as crazy as you think. They base it off of your take-home pay, and then no more than you can afford will be taken out. If you get a raise or your salary jumps up or down, the loan will follow. So, no surprises. It's customized for low-income people to survive and not go broke."

"Really, I didn't even know that is possible. Something to think about. I will call if things change."

She hopped in her car and pulled away with a different sense of delight. Thinking first of how to drive to her new job seemed difficult, but the relief of being hired outweighed the current worries. Also, to her happiness, her stomach acids were settled. Her mind then wondered whether they would have to move again and the challenges it would bring. So many questions ran through her mind, but she felt she had had a good day.

"Lord Jesus, thank you," she said as a smile arose.

As she was driving home, the grand idea of sneaking into a local fast-food establishment arose in her mind. Ordering a vanilla milkshake seemed like a dream.

She closed her eyes at the first spoonful of her milkshake; the delicious vanilla ice cream brought on instant bliss. As she stared out the car window at the beautiful mountain range, a slight tinge of guilt crept over her; she knew her kids would die for one of these tasty treats. Slowly enjoyed every spoonful and discarded the cup. *This will destroy all evidence of my tiny splurge.*

Virginia chuckled.

She checked the mirror and saw no evidence on her face, then looked down at her clothes, which were all clean. She returned her gaze to her reflection in the mirror and grinned.

Chapter 13

To Banning, We Go!

With the long year of 1972 behind Virginia and her six children, 1973 didn't seem much better. Acrimonious times challenged America as President Nixon's Watergate trial began, followed by his famous quote, "I'm not a crook!"

The World Trade Center was completed as one of the tallest buildings in the world, and Morton's TV dinners were thirty-six cents. Noted movies opened, such as The Sting and Deliverance. Andrew Lloyd Webber's Jesus Christ Superstar unveiled on Broadway. A nation-dividing law called Roe vs. Wade passed as the Sydney Opera House opened in Australia. The terrorist, known as the IRA, bombed British train stations at King's Cross and Euston. Crazy times flourished, and a single mom was doing her best to safeguard her children. She taught them to hope and pray for a better tomorrow and to remain optimistic to see promising days ahead.

Instantly, Virginia was mobbed with questions and praises about how much they liked the idea of moving. Greg asked if Charlie would still visit if we moved so far away, but Virginia pretended not to hear.

"Everyone will finish out the school year here. Then we will have a summer to adjust to the new house."

All jaws dropped, with the words, new house. They thought they heard wrong, as many stares were shared amongst the astonished listeners.

"Far out!" Cynthia and Greg yelled, and the rest followed suit.

On cue, Maureen's worry was written across her face. She opened her mouth to voice her concerns, but before she could utter a word, Virginia assured her that it was affordable.

"Now, tomorrow…" pulling out a set of keys and waving them around, "does anyone want to see our new, four-bedroom, two-bathroom house?"

The outburst of excitement brought a smile to Virginia. She always felt such warmth around her children. They always seemed to lighten the mood, find laughter and excitement with every challenge and were such a help in times of need. Maybe because of their youth and being naive to the world and its worries. Whatever it was, she didn't care; she just knew it brought her joy.

The move was extremely hard, but the kids' attitude never added to the stress. Sure, they had their usual complaints like any other. Still, instead of six whining brats, she had six able-bodied, humorous helpers ready for the task.

In the makeshift breezeway bedroom, joy rang through the older boys as if they were heading to Disneyland, which they couldn't afford.

That night, no one could sleep. The thought of their own mansion, unexplored terrain, and seeing trains up close made the boys doubt this was happening.

Greg rolled over. "Patrick, Patrick? Mom never answered my question. You know about Charlie. You think he'll visit us, you know, being so far away?"

"You say, you know, a lot. We won't be that far away. It's only thirty minutes from here. Besides, Charlie likes us. He'll come to visit," Patrick answered as he rolled over.

In the other bedroom, Paul whispered, "Keith, Keith? Are you sleeping?"

"No, I can't stop thinking about the house. We need to explore the cool train tracks, you know, the ones Mom told us about. Also, I want a dog." Keith pounded underneath the overhead bunk with excitement.

Paul laughed as their giggles soon rang through the walls, and their mom shouted, "Go to sleep!"

Burying their heads in their pillow, they burst out in uncontrollable amusement, and suddenly, Keith farted. That sent their laughter through the roof.

The sun rose, and many exhibited undereye bags and puffiness from sleep depravity, but none of that mattered. They were anxious to see their new town, house, and mountains Mom spoke of.

Driving over the foothills and through Cherry Valley, the long stretch down Highland Springs Road screamed of wide-open pastures; it took their breath away. Finally, barreling down the narrow street called Wilson, Virginia told them she heard the owner of the ginormous cow pasture were the Dysarts. They were long-time residents of Banning.

Their hearts leaped as they came across exquisite homes in Mountain Air Estate.

Cynthia yelled, "Wow, is this where our house is?"

Virginia glanced down and said, "No, those are way too luxurious."

Across the road were wide-ranging trails with a large wash running down the middle. Their excitement shot around the moon, knowing what adventures they would have.

Keith asked, "How much longer? Are we there yet?"

Virginia glanced in the rear-view mirror and put on her blinker. Down the humble street stood a church school with vast fields and open areas. Then their eyes bulged out as they stared at an abandoned building. The kids exploded with adventurous thoughts. Some thieves, bandits, and other mafia hitmen may be hiding their loot in those buildings.

"Look at all we can explore!" Patrick said. "We love this place already."

Beyond the old two-story relic, there were more open fields littered with pepper trees. Foothills and mountains everywhere. Deep drainage ditches and rows of eucalyptus trees overstimulated the children's quest for exploration. So much so that they almost forgot about their new house.

Virginia swerved the car around the last corner on the little street called 40th.

"Here we are!" she proclaimed.

The green-trimmed, light-green stucco house had a rock roof. Hardly waiting for the car to stop, they all wanted to be first to the door. Virginia reminded them of their manners, and they settled.

The vehicle was turned off, and they piled out. The weeds were taller than Keith and Paul, and they didn't care. To them, the tall weeds were a jungle full of tigers and venomous snakes.

Following the pathway to the front porch, they approached the house and peered through the window with awe.

San Jacinto and the San Gorgonian mountains hedge this small town of Banning, known for its Stagecoach Days celebration once a year. The Banning pass was huge, and the surrounding mountains stood ominously. The Pass was an old thoroughfare of the famous Bradshaw Trail during the gold rush days. And the dryer weather seemed to have healing properties for many who escaped humid climates.

The I-10 freeway sliced down the middle, heading east and west, and the small town of Beaumont and Cabazon surrounded Banning like bookends. If one drove east and passed the town, it would carry you to Palm Springs, the Coachella Valley, or even the famous and forgotten water recreation area in its heyday, the Salton Sea. It also served as a gateway to all deserts, high and low, and would even take you straight to Arizona.

The family of six only knew the quiet community of Yucaipa, with its retirement trailer parks and chicken farms, with no major highways, planes, or trains anywhere near it. But Banning would turn out to be noisily different.

With the freeway close, an airplane route above, and double train tracks running along the I-10, a steady hum of machinery, derailments, blown freeway tires, and train horns blaring at every intersection ruled day and night.

As Virginia unlocked the door, the living room was to the left, and the dining room and kitchen were to the right. Split down the middle was the most extended hall they had ever seen. Six mystery doors and cabinets shouted secret rooms and maybe hidden compartments.

The six of them looked for the green light. Virginia nodded. It was like waving a checkered flag at the Indy 500. Burning rubber, the race was on. They flew in, staring at every nook and cranny. They called out bedrooms and hid in every closet.

Cynthia came running from the back bedroom. "Mom, there are two bathrooms!"

"Far out!" Greg screamed as they piled into the tiny bath.

Keith and Paul speedily jumped in the tub too.

Virginia proclaimed, "Okay, line up!" She stood at the end of the hall. "Keith and Pauly, last bedroom on the left."

They dove into their room and began claiming sides.

"Patrick and Greg, next bedroom."

They, too, disappeared.

Mom headed to the third bedroom, and Maureen interrupted. Excitedly, she asked, "I know, me and Cynthia share this room!"

Virginia shook her head no. "This is your room and yours alone. You are my oldest, and you deserve it."

Virginia smiled as she pushed the door open for Maureen to see. Maureen stepped in and looked around; she was overwhelmed with joy. Her eyes began to tear. She turned and said, "But where are you going to sleep?"

"Cynthia and I will share the master with the bath. I guess we are used to each other," she replied, and Cynthia hugged her. "Also, I can get ready in the morning with my own bath. Now, go ahead. You've earned it."

Virginia embraced her girls, and the boys overheard Maureen being given her own room, and a chorus of "lucky" and "not fair" echoed throughout.

The euphoria subsided for a bit as the next question arose, "How do we move our stuff?" Patrick yelled, and a quick reminder to use the inside voice was issued.

"Charlie offered to rent a moving truck," Virginia said as she walked away.

The kids abandoned the inside rule and burst out with delight.

"Far out, can we ride in the truck with him? What's it like? Is it an eighteen-wheeler?" Greg danced around his mom.

"We move in two weeks. We'll have to get creative with school and me driving back and forth to work. So, listen up. I need you all to behave and help me. I cannot risk my new job for a runny nose, sniffles, or pouting, and especially injuries!" Virginia said, glaring at Paul. "You got it?"

"Loud and clear!" Patrick shouted as the younger brothers laughed.

The drive home for the family was surreal, as an unusual quietness settled. Paul stared out the window, wondering what treasures awaited in the old buildings and the new house. Keith thought of hiking and getting close to the trains. Patrick and Greg wanted to reach the foothills and explore and, of course, be the first. Cynthia wondered if there were neighbors to play with.

Maureen studied Mom. Her mind then wandered to what it would be like to have her own room and the generosity of her mom to give it to her. She couldn't help but feel slightly guilty for having her own room and her mother still sharing one. She knew her mother deserved it more than anyone. With this thought, Maureen opened her mouth to say something but stopped herself. There was no doubt in her mind that her mother would not waver in her decision. *You've earned it*, is what she said.

Her mother's words repeated in her mind. She then gazed out the window, feeling more blessed than ever before.

Virginia thanked God for making a way where there seemed to be no way. She pondered over the first Yucaipa move years ago, the new schools, and bone-jarring bus rides to work. A smile swept across her face at the thought of the free old car.

The smile quickly vanished as she remembered the unsettling layoff, which still left a sour taste in her mouth. But the bitter feeling quickly left because now, before her eyes and through prayer, struggle, and trials of life, it dawned on her that she now had a new job and house, and the kids were over-excited. *I did it! I can't believe that it's all working, God...thank you! It's all because of You. You guide my steps every day. Help me never to forget that.*

She smiled again.

Maureen caught her mother's smile out of the corner of her eye and couldn't help but feel proud. Virginia glanced at Maureen as if she knew exactly what she was thinking. Maureen smiled back and turned to look out the window once more. At that moment, everything felt right. But the moment didn't last long for Virginia. One more thought entered, and it was that of Charlie. What to do?

The time had come, the moving van arrived, and Charlie stepped out. A bombardment of kids mobbed him, and he quickly lined them up for duty. The army loaded the few items they had, and Virginia watched as he guided the kids with care.

Cynthia ran by and stopped. "Mom, we like Charlie so much. Will he visit us in Banning?" Before an answer was given, she scurried away to continue helping.

Virginia's eyes dropped, and she shook her head. She didn't have an answer to give, even if she wanted to. Heading inside, she packed the last of the kitchen. Deep agonizing thoughts again of not being divorced invaded her mind. *How on earth does one even file for divorce? How much does it cost? The thought terrifies me.*

She shook her head as hurtful scars suddenly peeled open. Fears soured her insides. Acids began a sweltering creep up her esophagus as her thoughts leaped to a horrible idea. *There could be, God forbid, custody battles, or I lose my children for good? I never paid for Pauly at the hospital? I can't let anyone take them away from me.*

Virginia exhaled, trying to calm herself down as she thought, *Virginia, you can never date anyone ever again! You are not divorced, and that's not right! Besides, I will need an annulment from the church. How on earth? You can't afford the price, and once again, another deep loss.*

Tears began welling in her eyes as she quickly suppressed her dilemma. She took a deep breath and thought of what to do with Charlie.

He was so wonderful to her and the children. He wasn't afraid of that responsibility, nor a coward; he only enfolded them like a father and friend. He had a way of keeping the boys in line and gentleness with her girls. *He is a good man. But...I find myself in a battle, trying not to fall in love with him. Which I think I might be. My heart cannot bear any more pain if something went wrong. Virginia, let him go! But it's been seven years since your husband left you!* She wavered. *Let…it…GO!*

While shouting in her mind, the kids poured in for another load. She escaped to the restroom to take another deep breath and gather her thoughts. She splashed her face with water and buried it in the towel. Uncontrollable tears poured out. She knew at that moment her feelings for Charlie were growing.

Soon, the moving vehicle was loaded, and the boys squeezed into the cab with Charlie. They had never been in such a huge truck. To them, this was the best day ever. Riding high and watching Charlie shift the gears was awesome. They felt like truckers, and their imaginations ran wild about long travels, touring unforeseen places, and C.B. radios.

Driving through the wash that separated Yucaipa from Calimesa, the road was narrow as they climbed. Looking over the edge, Paul was scared the truck would tip over and grabbed Keith's arm. Laughing, Keith pretended to tip over, and the brothers giggled. Paul laughed nervously with them, still gripping the seat.

Soon they were on the ten freeway, bouncing along, and the mountains of the pass came into view. Excitement grew in their new, uncharted territory. With the drive only twenty to thirty minutes away, it still felt long to the younger boys. And before they knew it, they backed into the driveway. The boys were shocked to see Mom and the girls already there.

"Not fair, the girls beat us!" Patrick protested.

"They took the secret route," Charlie joked.

Still young and gullible, Keith and Paul imagined secret tunnels of sorts. Both marveling at the idea of this, they piled out of the massive machine and ran wild to the house with the others. Halted by the traffic controller, also a police and interior decorator, Virginia demanded that no one enter empty-handed. Each had to carry a box or a piece of furniture.

"Pauly set that there. Greg, that goes in my room, and Cynthia, in the kitchen with that box."

The orders flowed like a well-orchestrated symphony. Soon the truck was almost empty, and the garage was scattered with leftover boxes. Then, Virginia made sandwiches for all.

After lunch, Charlie ordered the last thing to be brought into the house. The crowning jewel of all of Virginia's possessions…the old piano.

"Careful, careful with it!" Virginia voiced.

All members hoisted, steered, grunted, and pushed her prized piece through the front door and over the carpet to where she pointed.

"There, that's perfect. This old piano and I go way back, and I will never part with it."

Charlie opened the lid exposing the ivories. "Can you pluck a couple of keys for us? I've never heard you play."

"No, it will hurt your ears. I'm way too rusty." Virginia laughed, but all the children raised cheers for her to take a shot and play a few notes. Finally, she caved in. "Oh, all right, if this gets you off my back."

Sitting down and adjusting the bench, she slowly set both hands, and to all surprise, several beautiful chords lifted from the strings. Quietness settled on the listeners, and the kids were astonished that the piano could sound that good. They sat around, staring in awe.

Charlie stared with large eyes as if soaking in the melody. Quickly the tune ended, and all snapped out of their trance.

"That's it. Now back to work, everyone." Virginia stood and took a bow to huge applause.

The rest of the day was spent pulling, discarding, and sweating over the front landscaping. Suddenly, the fun was turning grueling and hot. Cuts and blisters began forming as they plowed down the weed monstrosity, and when Virginia stepped out, she beamed. It felt and looked like a different home. Their hard work paid off because the yard was now visible.

Thoughts of where to plant the first rose bushes played in her mind.

"I would like grass throughout the front. Alvera plants over there." She pointed to the south. "I would like thick hedges along the front window and my roses right here," she announced, dreaming of what it would look like.

She stood by the large dining window. Everyone paused, and they, too, imagined what it would look like. The thought that this home was theirs was settling in, and the blessing poured over them. It seemed surreal that they had their first home.

A small sense of pride swept over the older kids as they beamed at their mom's success. Maureen and Patrick stopped briefly and stared at their mom with a smile. There was a new sparkle in her, one they had never seen before. Even Charlie, still cleaning up the last of the weed piles, paused and watched Virginia as she planned her dream yard.

Her eyes scanned the yard until they caught Charlie's. This brought her back to reality.

Virginia's eyes hit the ground. Then she quickly headed into the house.

Charlie looked at the kids and grinned, then continued his task.

Chapter 14

Pioneer Town

Virginia's secret passions for Gene Autry and John Wayne fueled her love for the old west and men with broad shoulders. She fancied that someday one of these men would ride in on a horse and whisk her away. With very few television channels, once and a while, they would show a good western or thrilling monster movie on a Saturday featuring Godzilla, Gargantua, or King Kong. But Virginia's love was with John Wayne. She would encourage the boys to watch, so they could learn to be men, and they never objected. There was nothing like a good western.

However, Keith and Paul's deep passion was for sure with the monster movies. Their playtime was made up of constant attacks from giant beasts. Even the sky wasn't safe from Mothra, and they braced themselves for a strike from Monster Zero at any time.

Settling into the new home was smooth, and their outdoor playground was endless. They discovered acres of washes and ditches full of bike trails to the west. South, the older boys scurried across the busy Ramsey Street and ducked into giant drainage tunnels under the I-10 freeway. Two massive concrete passages that paralleled each other, littered with graffiti, led to the double train tracks. One more, shorter tunnel exited to the precipice of a deep wash, which seemed like the Grand Canyon. Patrick and Greg's jaws dropped with euphoria when they discovered this; the endless explorations that awaited them couldn't come soon enough. Quickly, they sprang down the drop on the old trail.

The wash led left, then opened to the right, lizards in abundance, crows fleeing at their sight, and an occasional snake scurried into the sage. Turn after turn, cliff after cliff, kept on forever. The wash headed farther to the open plains and the Idyllwild mountains' base. Arriving at a giant pipe stretching across the wash, they continued and found they were not alone. Several cows shared below and on top, circling a green waterhole.

As cows scurried past, Greg said, "Far out! We should build a boat and float in this lake."

"Greg," Patrick stared. "It's a cow toilet, full of pee and poop…that'd be gross."

Greg frowned, but deep inside, he knew his plan was genius.

While older brothers explored the southern frontier, Keith and Paul went up the street from their house and turned right on a short dead-end. Standing before them was a giant, two-story abandoned building with a wide-open loading dock. They hopped onto the top step. The first and second graders grinned at each other with excitement and fear. Their bravery was tested as they entered the large open room with tall, creaking rafters above.

They looked around and saw pigeons and owls droppings that littered the floors under their perch, and the other door to the east opened into the vast fields with paved roads lined with pepper trees. In the distance was a large Quonset hut structure.

"That's cool. Let's check it out!" Keith eagerly said, already making his way over with his little brother on his tail.

However, as soon as they walked through the small, opened warehouse, they halted. Peering to their left, they saw a dark hallway leading to what appeared to be old offices. A strange red tint left a ghostly aura in the alluring passage, and their imaginations began to run crazy.

"Cool!" Keith said as he pressed closer.

There seemed to be a magnetic draw that seized the explorers toward it. Chills crept up their spines as they inched forward into the haunted chamber. With Paul squeezing behind the safety of Keith's shadow, they snuck into the darkness, and the hall led left. The atmosphere was nearly pitch black, except for the reddish glow that lingered throughout.

Holding tight to where they stood, they waited until their eyes adjusted.

Maybe a hidden safe with cash awaits? Paul dreamed while Keith whispered, "Come on."

Slowly they went until a staircase appeared. Their thrill erupted because they loved stairs and different levels. Keith breathed deeply as he gripped the railing. He slowly lifted his foot as he took his first step up the rickety stairs. The creaking boards echoed off the tight walls and throughout the entire building. Both gritted their teeth as the noise rang out to their horror.

"So much for the surprise," Keith whispered, and Paul nodded in agreement.

Step after step creaked and moaned as they ascended to sheer death. The red glow had to be from splattered blood. They just knew it, a ghoulish monster would ravage them at any moment, but the closer they climbed, the lighter it became. Now, the reddish glow seemed to turn orange.

Anxiously, they anticipated the snatch of a creepy hand or swipe of a blade. Their curiosity ruled their fears. Finally reaching the landing and still alive, their eyes beheld an abandoned office. Their questions were immediately answered as to what caused the mysterious glow. Overhead, there were strange orange fiberglass slats serving as a roof cover, which caused the colored lights.

"Man...is that all it is?" Keith huffed, wanting something more sinister.

Their disappointment turned to delight when they saw old desks, cabinet doors, and dispersed papers littering the floor. Quickly looking for the hidden compartment containing oodles of stashed cash, they explored every nook and cranny.

"Keith, look at this!" Paul shouted as he opened the door to a balcony overlooking the hall below. "Far out!"

Thin rafter boards were holding up the roof, tempting Keith. "Look, I bet we can climb from here onto those boards, cool." Keith smirked as he scoped his possibilities.

"I don't know. Mom would kill us!" Paul replied hesitantly, looking down to the depths below and imagining Keith splattered on the concrete.

"What she doesn't know won't hurt her, will it? And don't be such a fathead!" Keith sneered.

"Stop calling me names, jerk!" Shrugging, Paul stated, "It's your life. I'm going to the other building."

He turned to leave, knowing it would divert Keith's quest of dangling on the timbers over the warehouse's concrete floor.

Quickly heading down the darkened stairs, their thrill was at an all-time high. They continued to explore, with a new venture around every corner. They loved Banning and its variety of exploration sites.

~

"Cynthia? Can you go find Keith and Paul?" Virginia asked.

Cynthia paused, thinking exactly where they might be. "Yes, I know where they are. I'll be right back."

She headed outside and walked up the street. *I wonder if there is anyone I can play with around here,* she thought as she looked at the few houses and empty lots.

Looking and the neighbors' front porches, she muttered, "I see some bicycles that look like they belong to girls…there's potential."

Reaching the end of 40th Street, she peered up at the old warehouse and saw Keith and Paul. Later they learned that this old building was also used as a dancehall.

"Hey, you two, Mom wants to take us on a drive. Come home!" she yelled.

"I'll race you!" Cynthia challenged.

"You're on!" Keith said as the boys raced Cynthia back to the house.

The two boys quickly faded because they were no match for Cynthia's long and smooth stride.

Their deflation of losing the race quickly disappeared. It was replaced with thinking of a drive, and just maybe, they would get a treat. Although rare, there was still hope.

"Everyone, in the car, we are going to Pioneer Town," Virginia said.

They eagerly loaded into the old Chevy. The motor fired up, thrills were ignited, and off they went to the freeway. *I wish we could go on more of these drives*, Virginia thought, knowing it was a rare event to splurge for her kids. She couldn't afford it.

Summer heat blew through the open windows across their faces, and they didn't care. All six kids stared at the approaching desert as they barreled into Cabazon. The average person may think there wasn't much to look at, but to the kids, adventure screamed everywhere. Even the small airport at the end of Banning was cool to them.

A billboard proclaiming date shakes at the Hadley store came and went. The older kids were wondering what a date shake was, let alone what a date looked like.

As she eased the gas pedal, Virginia suddenly called out for everyone to look left. They couldn't believe their eyes. A brontosaurus stood ominous. Its long neck reached the desert sky, standing on its four enormous feet, finished by the longest tail anyone had ever seen.

A gasp from all echoed through the car, then a chorus of, "Can we stop and see it!" rang from every voice.

Virginia calmly said, "Maybe on the way back."

"What is that place called, Mom?" Cynthia asked.

"The dinosaur is part of the old restaurant called, The Wheel Inn. Mainly truckers stop there," Virginia said.

"Cool, can we stop there?" Keith yelled.

Virginia just kept driving, and the chatter in the car elevated for the next thirty minutes of Dinny, the dinosaur—they later learned the behemoth's name.

As the miles rolled on, they headed into a narrow and steep canyon, which climbed to the Morongo Valley. The old Chevy roared up the last rise to Yucca Valley. The motor revved as strong whiffs of burnt oil billowed. Soon, one more left turn led the troops between massive and wondrous rock formations.

The kids thought it was maybe stacked dinosaur eggs. Smooth, brown, and oval shapes were abundant throughout the landscape. Formed shadows stretched along each stack of boulders, and the kids imagined playing with their holsters and cap guns on the rock tops.

Tall Joshua trees and yucca plants reached everywhere they looked, and stubby cacti dotted the ground.

"Those are barrel cactus, and if you are ever trapped in the desert, slice one open because they have water in the middle," Virginia pointed out.

Paul's jaw dropped in amazement, wondering how she knew that.

A dusty sign ahead read *Pioneer Town*. They turned on Roy Rodgers Road, and Main Street came into view. There stood the old ghost town, and they were in awe.

Virginia parked the Bel-Air and said, "Listen to me, don't touch the cactus, and look out for rattlesnakes." Her instructions were firm.

The boys flew out the doors, tempted by the immediate need to explore.

"Mom, can we walk around over there?" Patrick pointed to the wide-open area of untouched barren acres.

"Yes, you may, and watch your brothers," Virginia answered as she turned to the town, and the girls walked with her.

A freeing old-west spirit covered the area, and they all felt it. They fell in love with it immediately.

Searching around every bush and inspecting the barrel cactus, Greg shouted and pointed, "Look, a giant iguana!"

Speeding to the strange beast, Patrick corrected, "I think that's just a big lizard."

The creature darted away, and they were elated.

"You're wrong, Patrick. That was an iguana," Greg said.

They argued back and forth, and Keith and Paul didn't care what it was. They just loved seeing it and imagined keeping it as a pet and naming it.

Before they knew it, Virginia's whistle echoed off the rocks, and the boys moaned in disappointment; there was so much left to explore.

Greg ran to Mom and told her he saw an iguana, and Patrick rolled his eyes, waiting for Mom to correct Greg.

She said, "Yes, there are desert iguanas here."

Greg shouted, turning to his brother.

Patrick ignored him, and Paul was impressed again at how smart his mom was.

She continued, "There are also Gila Monsters. A unique lizard, usually black and orange in color. So, I will count you both correct."

"Mom, how did you know this town was here?" Maureen asked.

"It was an old Hollywood movie set. I know Gene Autry and Roy Rodgers started it in the late forties. They filmed a bunch of old western movies in this very spot," she said, pointing around to the town.

She beamed and said, "I've always wanted to visit."

Virginia entered a dream world of old movies, recognizing several areas she had once seen in her favorite films.

Maureen nudged her and asked, "Mom?"

"What? I'm just daydreaming about Gene Autry." She laughed as they walked down the old boardwalk.

"Who's hungry for an early dinner?" Virginia asked, and the kids were overjoyed that they got another rare treat.

They arrived at a large stucco building littered with many windows in the front with smaller, single panes.

Opening the large, ornate wooden doors, they were treated to the odd sound of bowling balls racing down wooden lanes. To their surprise, there was a small, six-lane bowling alley. It seemed so out of place in this little ghost town, and the kids thought it was the grooviest thing. Now seated, they were engrossed with the few patrons trying to roll their strikes. The kids had never bowled before, let alone seen an alley. They watched and wondered if the sport was easy. Before they knew it, cheeseburgers and French fries sat before them, and their own soda filled with ice.

Paul stared in wonder at his lunch basket. It was so tasty looking and rare to have this before him; it was hard for him even to eat it. He wanted it to last forever, but the whiff of hot fries and a grilled burger with melted cheese made his mouth gush with anticipation.

Watching her youngest gaze at his basket, Virginia asked, "Pauly, is there something wrong with your food?"

Paul shook his head, smiling as he naively looked from his basket to his mom. It seemed like a dream, but it wasn't. It was all his to eat.

Slowly reaching for the soft drink, he took his first sip. It cooled his mouth and coated it with delightful sugary pleasure. His insides smiled the largest they ever had.

Paul looked at his brothers and sisters as they silently plowed into their delicacies. Patrick held his half-eaten cheeseburger. Greg had several fries hanging from his mouth as Cynthia swung her legs while sipping her drink.

Maureen was proper, eating one French fry at a time, and Keith was spooning his grub into his mouth like he couldn't eat it fast enough. Paul laughed to himself. Again, it seemed like a wonderful dream. He felt rich and blessed. Reaching for his burger, he stretched his mouth as wide as he could as his taste buds exploded with flavor.

The meal seemed to last a long time. Every bite was consumed, and the never-ending slurping sound bounced off the old walls as they extracted every ounce of the soda pop. All felt their bellies were larger than they had ever been.

Virginia leaned back in her chair and looked at her children. Moments like these were when she felt peace, and seeing the joy on her children's faces made her life wonderful. Despite all the chaos, burdens, and struggles life dished out, those moments made life satisfying.

She closed her eyes, holding tightly onto this feeling of contentment. Then the thanks and hugs surrounded Virginia as they slowly rubbed their stomachs and chattered about their favorites.

As they began touring the town, Virginia slowly seemed to be controlled again by a dreamlike melancholy. All cultivated from her romantic love of the old west and Hollywood's handsome actors. A similar feeling poured over to her kids. They felt as if they had just time-traveled. The old false-front buildings stood tall, and saloon gun battles played out in imaginations.

Virginia pointed to more familiar areas she swore she saw in films. The boys mimicked cowboys threatening to make one-draw their pistols in a duel, and clink sounds echoed from their pretend spurs. Greg pretended to walk bowlegged down the dusty street. Virginia laughed at their creativity and excitement. Pioneer Town was everything she imagined it would be.

To their disappointment, she announced, "Well, cowboys and cowgirls, it's time we saddle up and drive off into the sunset."

With many protests and groans, they headed back to their stagecoach, the old Chevy.

Barreling down the twisting highway, Virginia thought what a thrill it was to visit the old town, and the laughter and stories didn't stop. She also thought, *Wow, no one got injured. We made it through one trip without an incident.*

"Mom," Maureen let out. "I think I'm going to be sick."

Virginia glanced over, saw how pale she looked, and thought, *Oh well.*

She calmly pulled over, and poor Maureen lost her lunch. Maybe the extreme heat and winding canyon roads were the culprit.

Pulling the Bel-Air back on the highway, they approached The Wheel Inn.

"Can we stop, Mom, please?" Patrick yelled from the back seat.

Virginia was silent and seemed nervous, staring at the dash gauges and then at the road.

"Mom?" Patrick asked as they flew past the brontosaurus.

"Mom?" Maureen could tell that she now showed massive worry.

The kids quieted, knowing too that if she was silent, then something was up.

Soon, entering Banning, the car smelled of burning oil and reeked of steam.

The kids were still looking out the window when a sudden *bang* shot through the hood of the car, followed by a terrible sound of unwanted pieces of metal bouncing inside the engine compartment.

The car sputtered as Virginia pulled to the side of the freeway as a colossal plume erupted, making it impossible to see. It was as if a smokestack from a factory was under the hood. But Virginia kept her calm and could easily park the dying car.

"Everyone exit out on the right side. Once out, follow me."

She crawled out of the passenger side because of the freeway traffic on the left. As they followed, the old car was still billowing its plumes and dripping unsavory amounts of water and oil. Stepping around the fluids, they stayed behind the leader as she led them off the freeway ramp.

They arrived at the nearest service station.

"Are you going to call Charlie?" Patrick asked.

"No, I'll call my brother," Virginia replied.

Stepping into the phone booth, still as calm as ever, she dialed her brother's number. The kids were silent. Only the older boys whispered. Everything was an adventure to them. Maureen, whose facial color was returning to normal, worried about the car and finding the money to fix it. Cynthia stayed close, silent, but listened to her mom's every word.

"Yes, hello, Lloyd, yes, we're fine. We broke down. Can you call Mom to pick us up? We're stranded. I don't really know how far we are from home, but I think we are close." A pause hung around until she said, "Thank you so much, goodbye."

An hour passed as they sat on the small wall of the service station, and soon, their grandma pulled into the parking lot in her large, blue Ford Galaxy. Following behind was Lloyd in his Ford pickup truck.

"Well, sis, you want the good or the bad news first?" Lloyd said through his window.

"Just give it to me straight." Virginia exhaled in exhaustion as she approached.

"Your motor exploded, and I mean exploded. There is a hole through your hood. Something shot straight through, and, sis, when you blow up a car, you really do a bang-up job!" He laughed.

"Well, you know me, I want to make sure I go out with style!" she joked as well, to the kid's amazement.

"I will call a tow truck. This one won't be coming home ever again. I will help you look for another vehicle. You head on home with Mom, and I'll call you in a few days when I find one." Lloyd smiled at the kids, and their eyebrows peaked at the thought of a new car.

"Thanks, Lloyd. Once again, you have helped me out of a bind." She reached in and patted him on his shoulder, and he drove away.

They piled into Grandma's car, and before they knew it, they were home.

"Gosh, Mom, if I would have known we were this close to the house, we could have walked." Virginia shook her head.

"Don't worry about it. It gave me another excuse to see my grandkids. You kids, make sure you take care of your mother, okay?" Grandma smiled, and hugs were in abundance before she left.

The kids told their mom what a fun day it was, and they were sorry about the car.

"Well, that's how it is sometimes. But it's how you persevere through it. The car served us well, and I guess it's time for a new one. Anyone excited to have a newer, I mean another, very used car? We can't afford a brand new one," Virginia said.

The kids cheered and threw in their suggestions for what type, but Virginia laughed at the requests for racecars and four-wheel drives. "Sorry, it has to be practical and affordable, and don't forget, needs to fit seven people. You all aren't shrinking either." Once again, she was right, as always.

After their showers, they went to bed and played back their visit to Pioneer Town, and each had their own story to keep forever. Patrick and Greg loved the lizards, cacti, and dangers of the desert. Maureen and Cynthia loved the movie aspect and the actors and actresses. Keith and Paul couldn't stop talking about the food and the bowling alley.

They dreamt about living there or having a bowling alley in their homes when they grew up. It was an adventure. Even though there was one sick kid, and the trip spelled the end of the old Bel-Air, the day was perfect.

Virginia washed her face and stared in the mirror. She, too, smiled and enjoyed the day. Closely following was a deep sigh as she thought, *How are you going to afford a car, Virginia? Good grief, does it ever end, and how am I going to get to work Monday? Sunday is tomorrow. Maybe I'll call Charlie and see if he can fix it. No, Virginia, let him go!*

Her insides twisted in anxiousness as she turned the light off and went to bed.

Chapter 15

The Red-Ryder BB Gun

The next day after the death of the Bel-Air was Sunday morning, and they waited for a call from their Uncle Lloyd. The living room floor had become a childhood re-creation of the Revolutionary War. The toy red and blue coats of plastic military men were lined for battle. With rubber bands in hand, the action commenced.

"We'll fight to the death!" Keith led the charge.

Paul was behind his soldiers, and the rubber bands flew. One by one, the tiny soldiers fell from the stinging pain of the flying rubber arrows. Soon, Paul's army was decimated. Keith claimed victory while half of his army still stood. Jealous, Paul threw a cushion at his survivors and wiped them clean.

"Cheater!" Keith yelled as he shoved Paul to the ground.

"Mom, Keith shoved me!"

From afar, Virginia yelled, "Keith, no roughhousing!"

He turned, and his eyes were ablaze as he held up his knuckles, and Paul repaid him by sticking his tongue out.

Keith said, "Tattletale!"

That morning was tiring for all after their fun day in Pioneer Town. Virginia was on the phone most of the morning, and to everyone's relief, she seemed excited.

"Wow, thank you, thank you, God!" Virginia hurried to her bathroom to change and freshen up.

The troops congregated until she appeared and announced, "Lloyd found us a car! He'll be here any minute. And before you ask, all I know is that it's the same color as the last. That's all I know before you drill me with a million questions. Now, go comb your hair and get dressed. You look like a buncha ragamuffins."

"Mom, how much will it cost?" Maureen asked the question that wasn't answered.

"This is another blessing from above, only a hundred dollars. But, before you stress, I can pay my brother back in payments. It's doable. So, don't worry."

Virginia started a pot of coffee, and there was a buzz in the house.

"You're on your own for breakfast!" she hollered as she went outside.

Paul ran to the window, and there it was, an immaculate and newer-looking car pulling in. It was longer than the last and more rectangular shaped. "It's here. It's here!" he shouted like Paul Revere.

Sprinting outside, they marveled.

"Here you go, Virginia. How do you like your luxurious car?" Lloyd laughed as he greeted her.

"It's beautiful. What is it? Is it an Oldsmobile?"

"Yep, a 1964, Ninety-Eight! Full power, I mean, everything. Electric windows, antenna, seats, you'll feel like royalty!" He turned to the boys, and his countenance changed. "You boys take care of this car and your mother, you understand me?"

The boys felt he was burning a hole through their hearts with his stare, and they all nodded in compliance.

"Good, glad we have an understanding."

While under the watchful eye of their uncle, they slowly entered the blue interior luxury, and it seemed like door-to-door buttons. So hard was the temptation not to push everyone at once. They tamed their curiosity. Patrick wisely asked if he could try a few, and Uncle nodded. The windows went up and down with the push of a button.

"Far out!" Greg shouted as the seat moved up and down as well.

Next, the antenna was the same. *How is this possible?* they wondered.

The car was nothing like their other, and this was like new—no rips, no stench of duct tape, and plenty of room to spare. The radio worked, and the sound was quality. Patrick pushed a button in the glove box, and they heard a *thunk*! Looking around, they wondered what had happened.

Keith shouted, "The trunk opened!"

They were astonished at the futuristic car. Their life had been so simple, and this car was far from simple. They sped out to look. The trunk was so giant that it defied imagination.

"Is there anything wrong with it, Lloyd?" To Virginia, it seemed too good to be true.

"Well, yes. The guy I bought it from said it's having transmission issues, I didn't experience anything, but he said once in a while, it slips and is hard to shift. Someday it will need to be rebuilt. I suggest just use it for an around-town car, easy trips, and be light on the throttle. The price was right."

"Yes, the price is right, and I'm very thankful…would you like some coffee?"

They went inside, and the kids went nuts in the car. Touching everything except Maureen, she left and joined the grownups.

Patrick found a flap in the trunk, which they knew was a secret compartment. Opening it revealed the spare tire, and below it, Patrick's eyes bugged as he saw something that excited him. Jumping in and reaching, he pulled out a hidden military bayonet resting in its sheath.

They gathered around the tantalizing weaponry as he slid the blade free. They were in awe of the cold steel of the past and imagined what battles it must have seen.

"Cool, there is even dried blood on the edge of the blade," said Patrick as he spun the blade in the light.

Patrick was in a trance, and Greg begged to hold it. Waving everyone back, Patrick headed onto the grass. He slashed the blade into the air as if a war had broken out. The kids jumped into the moment, acting like they were being stabbed and dying, until they heard, "Patrick!" Mom and Lloyd rushed outside.

"Look what I found in the trunk!" the wielding soldier yelled.

"Let's see that. It sure looks genuine." Lloyd held it, explained how it attaches to a rifle, and complimented what a great find it was.

"Can I keep it, Mom?" Patrick begged.

"All right, but do I need to remind you how dangerous it is?" Virginia said.

"I promise to be safe."

His uncle gave him the blade back. Patrick sheathed it, then passed it around. This excellent addition would sit well with the BB and pellet gun arsenal the older boys already collected.

~

Christmas was around the corner, and this would be the first in the Banning home. They set up their very thin, hand-me-down, shabby fake tree. Virginia set down a large bowl of unbuttered popcorn and a bag of cranberries, and each child had a needle and thick thread. The teacher began weaving the two together. Soon, a rhythm was struck, and their components grew longer. To their surprise, the edible garland began to look like Christmas. It was a beautiful strand of bright white and deep crimson.

The kids started to wind it around the bottom branches heading upward. A few hours passed, and after distributing band-aids from several pricks, they stood proud as they stared at the beauty of their hard labor.

Soon, the bulbs were up, and their mother's crown jewel was lots of tinsel. With the plug of the lights, the shabby tree transformed into a pretty and humble reminder of Christmas, and the kids were proud.

With the thrill of very few presents and the love of the holiday break, the early sunsets and, for once, colder weather kept the kids inside.

The level of roughhousing grew to new heights. While Maureen and Cynthia played it cool, listening to music, Patrick and Greg were wrestling on the beds in their room. Keith and Paul played with their cars under the tree, and Paul always seemed to anger Keith with his smart mouth, knowing his mom would always bail him out.

They decided to abandon the Matchbox euphoria and start a lively game of tag.

Keith shoved Paul to the ground and yelled, "You're it!"

He sped down the long hall and darted into the older boy's room, interrupting Patrick and Greg, who were now talking about hunting. They were holding their two rifles. One was a Red Ryder BB gun, and the other a pellet gun.

As Keith sped in, begging them to protect him from getting tagged, Patrick yelled, "Get out of our room, idiot!"

Setting the guns in the corner, Greg began to push Keith out as Paul sped around the corner. Keith wiggled from Greg's clutches and lunged for one of the rifles. Clutching the Red Ryder and aiming at his pursuer, Paul grabbed the other and pointed it back at Keith's stomach.

"Put those away, twerps!" Patrick yelled again at the nuisances.

Keith replied, "No, I need to stop him!"

He aimed the gun two inches from Paul's left eye, and BANG! The gun went off, and Paul's head snapped back as the stinging BB hit his left eye...down he went. Keith stood frozen as Paul fell to the ground with another familiar, blood-curdling scream.

Greg sped from the room to alert their mother, but she was already sprinting down the hall. She rushed in and saw Paul rolling on the ground, screaming and in tears, and Keith standing there stunned, holding a BB gun in his hand. She quickly realized what he had done.

Patrick ripped the gun from his hands, and Keith looked lost.

"What did you do, Keith?"

Virginia reached down and picked Paul up. She led him while he whaled from the pain.

"Maureen, grab my purse and get dressed! Kids take care of Keith. He's in shock. I'm rushing Pauly to the hospital."

Cynthia asked, "So what happened?"

Patrick and Greg delivered every detail. Keith sat by the tree, sobbing as Virginia and Maureen rushed the injured out the door and into the car.

Virginia, Maureen, and wounded Paul arrived at Pass Hospital in the late evening. They quickly rushed Paul in while Maureen was crying with worry. Virginia told Maureen, "Listen, I am dealing with Paul only, not both of you. You are supposed to be helping, so get it together!"

The night doctor asked Paul to calm down as they inspected his eye. His sobbing settled to a whimper.

As the doctor turned on her light, she said, "Now, let's see what happened. It looked like the BB bounced off the eye, and I think…" She stretched the eyelid out and down rolled the cold BB.

Paul felt it plummet off his cheek.

"It looks like the point of impact was here on the lower lid. See the bruise?" She pointed. "Then, as you can see the damage on the eye, here is where it ricocheted. You can see that the eye is in trauma. There are two excellent eye doctors, Slaney and Tarter. I will call to see who's available. I'll return in a few."

Virginia nodded as the doctor left. She looked at Paul lying on the gurney. Softly, she brushed his hair from his forehead and remembered when she gave birth to Paul alone. After that moment, she felt she always needed to protect her baby.

But trouble seemed to follow him. From birth, he would be the one always hurt or the one to break the other kid's toys, even their bicycles. The rumor was out that if Paul asked to play with one of your things, to say a big fat no!

In Yucaipa, Paul borrowed the only bike they shared and taught himself to ride it at six years old. But the cost was crashing several times to get it right, resulting in a broken gooseneck, which there was no money to repair. When he borrowed small toys, he stepped on or bent them in ways he thought were viable, only to render them broken forever. So, this stigma followed him. Now, here he was, BB to the eye.

"Oh, Pauly." Virginia sighed heavily as she thought of a little while back when the doctors stitched his forehead from the other tag accident.

Virginia began to fume. *Tag, tag, mothers of the world should outlaw that stupid game.*

"Where's Maureen?" Paul whispered.

"She won't stop crying, so they wouldn't let her in." Virginia's face looked sleep deprived.

"I'm sorry, Mom," Paul said as tears began to pool in his eyes again.

"Oh, Pauly, don't be. It was an accident. Keith is sorry as well and very scared for you."

Oddly, for some reason, he was comforted knowing that Keith felt remorse. He pretended it was a stomach punch that Keith deserved.

Then, a fearful thought struck him. "Will he go to jail for this?"

"No, you don't go to jail for roughhousing. Although, that may not be a bad idea to get you, kids, in order sometimes." She sternly smiled.

Still young and gullible, Paul sunk at the thought and feared that she might allow the police to haul them off. Before his imagination could get the better of him, the doctor reentered the room.

"Okay, we will be moving him to Redlands Community Hospital. I spoke to the eye doctor; he will meet you there. Do you want him to go by ambulance, or do you want to take him?"

Paul watched his mom's eyes enlarge, knowing this may be more serious than she thought.

She looked down at Paul and sighed again. "I'll take him."

It was now late at night, and exhaustion showed on his mom's face. Even at his young age, he could see how much these incidents seemed to take their toll on her.

"Do we go to the emergency room?" Virginia asked.

"No, there is a small office complex to the right of the hospital. There you will see the eye doctor. After he sees Paul, you will go across the street, where Paul most likely will stay a few nights."

"Stay the night?" Panic rang in her voice as the thought of work, driving, fuel, and the lack of money drove her worry deep into her bones.

"Okay then." She turned to Paul and said, "Did you hear that? You might have to stay a few nights."

To Virginia's surprise, Paul's expression changed to something of excitement.

Stay the night in a hospital? How cool! Paul thought this was the ultimate. Talk about getting some attention for once.

After putting a large bandage over the entire eye, they sent them on their way.

They pulled into the complex, and Paul shouted, "Mom, I don't feel very good."

"Maureen, hurry, let him out!" she shouted because Paul was sitting between them in the front seat.

Maureen shot out and took his hand to help him out of the car. It was just in time because his entire dinner and maybe lunch spewed across the parking lot.

"Oh, Pauly, you're traumatized." Virginia pulled some tissue and wiped his mouth.

Paul wondered if maybe he wasn't as well as he thought. Suddenly, everything hurt and felt weird as dizziness swirled. The thought of a hospital bed now sounded frightening.

They met the eye doctor out front and were quickly escorted in. He thoroughly examined the injury using various lights and stared deep into the damage zone.

He finally said, "The eye has filled with blood. We will need to keep him in the hospital until the blood recedes."

"How long does that usually take?" Virginia's worry just hit an all-time high.

"Could be a day or two, or weeks, depending on the damage." He motioned for Virginia to step away from her children for a private talk.

They stepped out, and he began, "The truth is, he will either heal from this, with damage or…" He paused, staring at her. "Virginia, he could even lose sight in that eye for good. Do you understand me?"

Virginia slowly looked over at Paul, at Maureen's worried face, then down to the ground. *Oh God, give me the strength.*

She steadied her breath and answered, "I understand."

"I'm sorry, he's young, and he may pull through just fine. But only time will tell. I'll meet you across the street. Head over, and they will check him into his room." He led them out and then departed.

Virginia tried her best to hide her worry as she approached Paul. She placed her hand on his shoulder and said, "Well, let's get you to the hospital. They have a bed waiting for you."

Sadness read across her face no matter how hard she tried to hide it. She hated having her kids see her worry, even worse, seeing her sad. She always wanted them to look at her and feel comforted. Virginia knew she had to leave him tonight. She wasn't sure how he would react but would soon find out.

The nurses checked Paul in, and he had to undress and wear a strange gown. It was close to midnight, and they laid him in his bed. With only a curtain separating him from the other unknown youthful and injured kids, Paul was too tired to notice or fuss. Still feeling ill from the whole affair, he desired to sleep. But before that could happen, the eye doctor, as promised, met them and thought it best to bandage both eyes for now. It was a strange feeling for Paul having his sight stripped away, but he was so tired that it didn't bother him. Paul lay there with his eyes covered in a darkened world and fell asleep.

"I'm tired," Virginia said to Maureen as she stepped out of the car when they arrived home.

It was now 1 a.m. They unlocked the door, and the other four children were asleep around the tree and on the couch, waiting for any news. They quickly sprang awake and approached Virginia. They looked past their mom and Maureen for Paul.

Patrick asked, "Where's Paul?"

Immediately, Keith thought the worst of it. Sobbing, he ran to Virginia's arms.

"Oh, it's okay, Keith." Hugging him tightly, she said, "He has to stay in the hospital because they need to keep a close watch. His eye is full of blood, and they need it to drain."

Greg asked, "Is he blind?"

"We hope and pray that it heals, but..." She paused and looked at Maureen because this would be the first time she heard this next bit of news. "There is a chance that he may lose sight in that eye, but the doctor is hopeful, and so am I."

Scared looks were exchanged among the worried siblings.

"So, how many nights does he need to stay in the hospital?" Cynthia asked.

"Could be a day, a week, or more. We don't know." Their mom let out a huge yawn. "I am glad it's Friday night because I'm exhausted."

"No, it's not. It's Saturday morning," Cynthia quickly corrected her.

"Okay, smarty-pants, you all get to bed; maybe I can take you to see Pauly tomorrow. Get going."

She hugged, and off they went, except Keith, whom Virginia had him stay back so she could talk to him alone. She bent down, so she was eye-to-eye with him. "Listen, it was an accident. Don't let it eat you up." She wiped away the tears that rolled down his cheeks. "How about you stay with your brothers tonight? You can sleep on the floor between their two beds. I don't want you to be alone tonight, okay?"

Keith managed a slight smile and wiped his remaining tears. "I'm so sorry, Mom."

"I know you are. And so does Pauly. Goodnight, I love you," she said as she ushered Patrick and Greg into Paul's room.

They came and enfolded him, then led him to their room.

Virginia went to bed and stared at the ceiling, thinking of her baby in the hospital alone. *God, be with Pauly. Please help him to recover and be able to see out of his eye. In the name of the Father, the Son, and the Holy Ghost, amen.*

Virginia fell asleep.

~

Beep, beep, beep, went the monitor from outside his room, waking him from his slumber in total darkness. He wondered where he was. *Why is it so dark? Is it night still?*

His hands rose to his eyes. He felt the patches, a fear began to overwhelm him, and he thought to yell for his mom. But a sudden thought took over, *No, I have to be brave.*

He breathed in and out, trying to calm himself down from the sudden shock. Then, he realized another issue arose. He had to pee something fierce. *Hmm, I really have to pee.*

He vaguely remembered what the nurse said, "Press the button" by his hand.

Feeling around, he found it.

The nurse appeared, and her stern voice was startling. "Yes, Paul, what do you want?"

Hearing her squawk and imagining an unpleasant face, Paul stated, "I have to use the bathroom, please."

"Okay, here is a pan. Just lay there and go in it, and I will remove it when you are finished."

"What? I have to pee in a pan?" Paul was shocked, and only being a second grader, he thought, what a strange world. "Does my mom know I have to potty this way?"

"Yes, you'll be fine. That's how it's done in hospitals," the nurse affirmed.

"What if…" A little embarrassed by this question, Paul lowered his voice. "What if I have to go number two?"

"It's the same," she said.

Paul scoured his face with his tongue hanging halfway out. "That's gross!"

The nurse slid the frigid pan between his legs. "Here it is. Do you feel it?"

Paul let out, "Ah, that's cold!"

"Okay, call me when you're finished." She closed the curtain and walked away.

Paul's imagination was leading to suspicions that she was still there. He tilted his head this way and that, trying to peer through his bandages but could see nothing.

He whispered, "Are you here? I don't want you to watch."

He waited and only heard the usual clatter of hospital life. He strained to go, but the oddity rendered his bladder useless. The sudden urge came and went, and nothing. Pressing the button, the nurse came in.

"Are you all finished?"

"No, I'm sorry, I can't go." Paul awaited an answer, hoping for mercy.

"Well, I can come back."

"Can I use the real bathroom?"

"Nope, doctor's orders are that you're to stay put."

"But I can't go in the pan. It's too hard."

"Well, when you really have to go, then you will."

Paul furrowed his brow in frustration and thought, *I pout at home, and it sometimes works. I'm not peeing in a pan.*

He crossed his arms and gave the silent treatment. It didn't work at home, and now he learned it had the same effect in the hospital…*Bummer.*

So, he fell back to sleep.

Early the next day, a voice said, "Good morning, Paul, I'm nurse Michelle, and I will be helping you today. How are you feeling? I brought you breakfast."

Waking again, still in darkness, he felt as if his bladder would burst. "Good morning. I really need to use the bathroom, but I can't go in the pan. I tried all night, but it doesn't work."

He slowly sat up.

"Well then, let's get you to the restroom. I will guide you." She touched his hand and lowered the bedrail.

Paul thought, *Yes, she's my guardian angel.*

He liked her voice more than the last nurse and especially liked what she had to say.

She helped him down, to his delight, but he felt like his inners would explode. As she quickly led him, he thought it strange not being able to see.

She closed the door, and he felt he unleashed a torrent. To his relief, he could breathe again. Probing his way to the sink, he washed his hands, found the door, opened it, and called for the nurse. She was waiting to lead him back.

She set his breakfast in front of him on a tray. "Okay, Paul, I will feed you."

The nurse sat next to him and prepared to spoon everything in.

Paul couldn't believe it; all this attention was paid to him. A rarity in his household. He sat up, and she shoveled it in, calling out what was on the spoon.

He ate to his delight.

Then she said, "Here's a straw for your milk."

As he slurped, his tastebuds screamed with joy. "Wow, this is milk? It's yummy."

"Haven't you had milk before?" she asked.

"Not this kind. My mom gives us powdered milk. She mixes it because I have a lot of brothers and sisters."

Curious, Michelle asked, "Paul, how many do you have?"

"There's six of us."

"Wow, your mom and dad sure must be busy."

"Just my mom...she takes care of us."

"A single mom with six kids? Good gracious. And where are you in the chain?"

"In what chain?" Paul said, thinking of a bicycle part.

"You know, are you the oldest, middle child?"

"Oh, I'm the baby." Embarrassed, he meant to say youngest.

"Wow, far-out. Well, your mother must be an incredible woman. What a good job she's doing. You're a very polite young man."

"Thank you," Paul said as she exited.

His belly was full. He turned over and listened to all the familiar sounds, waiting for the one recognizable voice he missed dearly.

~

Early that morning, Virginia rolled out of bed and stumbled to the bathroom. *Is that breakfast I smell and coffee?*

After washing her face and dressing, she went to the kitchen, and sure enough, the kids were up and prepared Mom a meal. They sat her down and set the table. Eggs and fried spam were on the plate with toast. The coffee was piping hot and made to perfection.

"You guys are wonderful, and your timing is spot on. Thank you."

After eating, they asked how they thought Paul was doing, alone in the hospital.

"Well, we haven't had a call, so I imagine he's hanging in there. I'm leaving as soon as I'm ready."

The kids jumped up as if to go, but she had to slam on the brakes on their ambition and explain hospital rules. "I know you're all wanting to go. Unfortunately, I'm the only one who they will let in this morning. Visiting hours are afternoon. That is the only time you can see him. Also, only two at a time. There's no way they will allow all of you at once, can you imagine?"

Greg responded with a loud "Hey!"

"I'm only kidding." She laughed. "Thanks, gang, this was needed. Now, I'm going to call my mother and sister to let them know about Pauly. So please keep the noise down."

After her chores were finished, Virginia pulled out of the drive, headed to the hospital, and used the precious moments to ponder and pray. *Lord Jesus, thank you for my job, and that I can afford insurance, I feel much better this go-around, last time, I never paid for Pauly. And I now know they won't take my children. It was silly of me to think they would in the past. But that's the way the ball bounces. You are my only hope and strength. I am so glad in this life, I have a heavenly Father. One who always looks after me and forgives and understands me. Really, thanks for always being there. In the name of the Father, the Son, and the Holy Ghost, amen.*

Checking into the hospital, she walked into the large room with several curtains until she found him. There he was, her baby, awake and sitting upright. He was alone with a large bandage on each eye.

Poor Pauly. She shook her head. "Good morning."

Paul jumped with excitement. His heart missed her deeply. He had never been separated from her and quickly realized he didn't like it.

"Mom!" he shouted as he held out his arms, waiting for her hug.

She squeezed him, and he loved her scent.

"Mommy, I had free breakfast and real milk, and they wanted me to pee in a pan."

"Slow down, Pauly."

"Sorry, they have real milk here." He beamed.

"Yes, most people don't have to mix their milk with powdered milk like we do. You're so sheltered, it seems."

"What's sheltered?"

"It just means as you grow, you will get out into the big world and learn many things are different than how we live."

"But I like the way we live."

"I know you do. You make sure you enjoy the milk and mind your manners." She patted his hand.

Just then, the doctor and nurse walked in.

"Good morning. How are we doing today?" he bellowed and stepped next to his patient. "I am going to peel back your left bandage and use my light to have a look. This won't hurt a bit."

"Ouch, that hurt!" Paul grimaced.

The sticky bandage felt like it was ripping his skin apart.

"Sorry, yes, these are sticky for a reason. We don't want you sneaking a peek. We need both eyes to rest. Now, let's have a look…hmm. All right, I see…" Peering into the damage, he shook his head. "Nothing's changed. Looks the same as last night. Still, there's heavy trauma. Looks like he will have a few more days here."

The doctor stood and addressed Virginia. "I know it's an inconvenience, but we need to watch him closely, and he has to rest both of his eyes. We don't have enough info about this kind of damage to send him home, and the frequency of BB gun accidents in the eye really is not that common. I will be in this afternoon, then one more time tonight." Turning to Paul, he said, "You just rest, okay? Please don't strain your eyes."

Paul nodded at the voice, and the doctor left.

"Well, Pauly, it looks like we are in for the long haul."

"It is? How long is the hallway?"

Virginia chuckled at this. "Silly, Haul, H.A.U.L., not hall. Meaning, you will be in here a long time, a long haul." Mom smiled, and so did the nurse.

"Oh…I get it." He was still trying to understand, but he didn't.

"I am letting Paul get up and use the restroom. He doesn't do well with the bedpan. That's our little secret. I will let the evening nurse know, as well. Besides, most people can see what they are doing. His situation just makes it harder. You're doing good, Paul." The nurse patted his hand and left the room.

"Your brothers and sisters, say hello. They miss you."

"Did Keith get a whipping?"

"Pauly! No, he didn't. He feels bad enough for this."

"I'm sorry. I'm glad he didn't get in trouble." Deep down, he thought, *Bummer, he deserved a whipping*, but only selfishly.

Then a wave of guilt hit him, knowing he, too, was holding the other gun, pointing at Keith's stomach. "Mom, I'm sorry for aiming the other gun at Keith."

"Well, I had a stern talk with your older brothers about keeping their guns out and loaded with BBs and pellets. If it was the pellet gun, your eye would be destroyed. Also, the BB ricocheted off your lower eyelid and bounced off your eye. So, it wasn't a direct hit. That's a good thing if you can find something good in all of this."

"Mom, I love you. You're the best mom in the world."

He reached out again and held her. Her presence alone was all the comfort he needed.

During visiting hours, their aunt and grandma brought the rest of the siblings, and two by two, they would get to visit. First, Virginia brought Keith in alone, and when he saw Paul's bandages, worry and fear were written on his face. Dropping his head and clutching Mom's hand, he wondered how serious the damaged eye was.

As if she was reading his mind, she said, "It's not as bad as it looks."

But Paul, still sour that Keith didn't get a whipping, laid back as if he was not that alert, trying to milk the moment to make Keith feel more guilty. Pretending not to hear them enter, he faked asleep.

"Pauly, your brother Keith is here." She nudged him closer.

Paul pathetically whispered, "Mom, is that you?"

Clearing her throat, she issued a stern warning, "Yes, Pauly, you know it's me. Now sit up. Say hello to Keith!"

Paul knew that voice all too well, and it was screaming, *Knock it off!*

"Paul, I'm sorry for what happened. Does it hurt?" Keith's voice quaked.

"It sort of...stings." That was the truth. "But I'll be all right. They make you try and pee in a pan while in bed."

"They do? How funky." Keith's demeanor changed.

"I can't, though, so they let me pee in the bathroom."

"Pauly, don't you have anything to say to your brother?" Virginia could always spot kid diversions, and she quickly sliced through it.

"Keith, I'm sorry for pointing the gun at you."

"That's cool. Accidents do happen." He strained a smile at his mom, and she frowned.

"But these accidents won't happen again, right?" She now set down a new law. "Last time you played tag, Pauly ended up with stitches. This time, he almost lost an eye. You boys need to guard and protect each other. We are all we've got. No more hurting one another, is that understood?"

Both boys nodded. When she spoke like this, it was clear she meant business, and the boys knew they had better obey.

"Now, when these accidents occur, who has to do all the work, driving, worrying, and praying that she can afford the bills that follow? Who loses sleep when she should be resting for work? Do you see the big picture in what these dilemmas cause? Now, Pauly, when the rest enter, you will be polite, and there will be no faking."

Paul lowered his bandaged face and complied. Nothing got past their mom.

One by one, each sibling visited and thought it cool that he got to wear bandages and was waited on hand and foot, with free meals to boot! But to Virginia's grief, there was still the news that had not been good for Paul's eye. Worry boiled at the fact that he may be blind in one eye, and the doctor confirmed no change.

One week moved at a snail's pace, and Paul was still in the hospital. Christmas was eight days away, and there was still no change.

Alone at night, the nurse entered and cleared Paul's dinner. "Would you like me to turn on the television? I think there is a Christmas program. It's...Rudolf, the Red Nose Reindeer."

Paul leaped up with joy but then sank because he couldn't see it. "Yes, please."

Soon, there was the show jingle, and Paul waited until the nurse left. Quickly, under his good right eye, he began to peel the bottom bandage. Laying on his right side, he found a spot where he could sneak a peek. Thrills and excitement fed through his right eye, knowing he got to watch Rudolf, yet horrible guilt pulsed, thinking he could destroy his vision.

For the next hour, a sense of therapy filled his soul. Being surrounded by such a sterile white and noisy environment, with dangling curtains, beeping monitors, flashing buttons, and intercoms, he felt like, truly, a glimpse of Christmas had arrived.

When the show was over, he heard the nurse coming, and he pressed the bandage and laid back, and the nurse entered.

"Well, Paul, did you enjoy it?"

Sitting up, he said, "Yes, thank you."

"Sorry, you couldn't watch it." She turned off the TV.

"That's okay. I'm glad I got to listen." He was laughing on the inside at his secret and successful mission.

On day eight, the doctor checked Paul's eye early in the morning. Peeling off the bandages, he had him keep his eyes closed until he asked. "Okay, please open your left eye."

Taking his light, he shined it into the damage and said, "Well, well, Paul, the eye looks like it's draining. This is what we have been hoping for. How do you see out of it?"

"It's good, I think." Though young, Paul was very thankful. "Wait, it seems a little blurry."

"Okay, we can deal with that…hopefully with glasses, at least you can see, that's a good sign. We will keep your left eye bandaged still, but your right eye will remain free. Do you like that idea?"

"Yes, thank you." Paul grinned with relief.

At the end of week two, Virginia and Paul waited for the doctor.

"Hello Virginia, are you happy to hear your son gets to go home in time for Christmas? We are confident that there will be no blindness."

Relieved, Virginia said, "Oh, thank God, and yes, thank you so much."

"Paul's eye is drained, now there is serious damage inside, and the drawback is that we will need to see him every day for the next several months." The doctor stared.

"What? How on earth will I get him to your office every single day? I just started my new job, and, well, what about after work?"

"Sure, after work is fine. The good news is the office is near you, across from the hospital in Beaumont. There are two of us doctors at the clinic, and we will make it happen. I know how tough it will be for both of you, but we also have a question for you two. This injury can be helpful to the medical field. Would you mind if several young students and doctors see your injury? This will be helpful to them as they treat others like you. What do you say?"

Paul looked at his mom, and she looked at him. She said, "I don't see why not. We always say, as mothers, don't shoot your eye out! Well, since now that it happened, if it's helpful, I don't see why not. Pauly, what do you think?"

Paul nodded, and the doctor was thankful.

"Great, here is what you can expect. When you come for your exam, there will be a few students and doctors each day, for a week or two, will look into your eye, and that's all."

"What's in there?" Paul asked.

The doctor smiled. "Good question. They want to see what impact injuries to the eye look like. It's hard to describe but imagine little shreds. Some of the damage is floating around in there as well. Also, we will have to check for glaucoma, and again, you will most likely need glasses. Thanks again. Your willingness to help will teach others." Opening the curtain, he said, "Well, Paul, are you ready to go home and enjoy Christmas?"

Paul discarded the shackles of a hospital bed and gown only to learn the orders extended to stay in bed at home for the next three weeks. His heart sank, knowing his bed was in the back bedroom, and he would miss everything during Christmas, but at least he would be home. He tried to be thankful, but it was hard.

Happily strutting out of the restroom, finally wearing his normal clothes, relief showed brightly on his face. He hated the hospital gowns, which left his fanny exposed.

A few days before Christmas, they walked out. It seemed forever that he had been away, and he was ecstatic to see the outdoors. With still a bandaged eye, he looked everywhere at the mountains, trees, birds, cars, and even street signs.

One of the most privileged things was riding in the front seat. Maureen sat in the back and let Paul have the important front seat, the passenger side window.

Soon, they pulled into their driveway, and Paul was greeted by his family. They seemed to be giggling, and Paul didn't know why. Until he stepped into the house, and there in the living room was his bed. Virginia already knew he would be bedridden, by doctor's orders, and no playing, so she had the boys move his whole bed, facing the Christmas tree.

He ran and jumped on it with total thankfulness, and Virginia's scream was blood-curdling. "Paul Wesley La Canfora! What on earth are you doing!"

Paul slumped down. "I'm sorry, I, I'm just excited to be home. Sorry."

Virginia was saddened. "I'm sorry too. Welcome home Pauly, and Merry Christmas."

Chapter 16

Abuse of Power

When any of the six children were shown individual attention, it felt like a burst of temporary fame. Virginia taught them to treat these few events in life with humility and thankfulness. During these few brief moments, their character showed either good or bad. When it showed good, Virginia beamed with pride. But, one time, the fame was mistreated as an abuse of power, and the other siblings knew it, which was bad.

Hot on the heels of the great BB gun caper, Christmas arrived. There were few gifts for all, but the consensus was that they were thankful Paul was seeing and recovering. Virginia ordered the children to be at his beck and call. After being waited on hand and foot by nurses for two weeks, Paul was happy as ever, but something drastically changed in him. Maybe Virginia was at fault for what happened next, but the blame their mom would say was clearly on Paul's shoulders. What blame, you might ask? Well, it all started when the runt of the family realized that since childhood, when he wanted something and asked, his siblings mostly responded with, "Get it yourself!"

Since Virginia ordered his bed to sit in the living room, and the doctor's orders were that he shouldn't exert himself, Mother demanded that they served Paul's requests with no bickering.

At first, the camaraderie was strong, and all were eager to help nurse Paul back to health. After Christmas, Paul was in bed, including a hospital stay for almost four weeks. And the willingness to help him began to lessen in his siblings.

One morning, Paul woke up and found his older brothers already watching television. He was upset because he wanted to watch his favorite program, but the boys were already watching theirs. With few channels, there wasn't much to choose from. However, he saw a golden opportunity to abuse his power. His veins began pulsing with control.

Figuring a way to stifle their amusement, he blurted out, "Hey guys, can one of you bring me a bowl of cereal? I'm hungry."

They ignored him because they didn't want to miss their show.

Again, he asked, "Greg, Patrick, will one of you please get me a bowl of cereal?"

Aggravated by the litany of requests Paul had already dished out, they quickly grew tired of the little tyrant.

Patrick looked fierce. "You can wait until a commercial. You won't starve. Don't ask again, or you'll get it!"

Furious, Paul sat up and returned, "I'm telling Mom. You are supposed to help me."

He got out of bed and headed to the kitchen to get his cereal.

Just then, Virginia came from her bedroom and found Paul out of bed in the kitchen. Patrick and Greg were watching TV and not helping, and fire poured forth.

"Pauly, I told you to ask for help. You need to stay in bed!"

"I did ask for help, but they wouldn't." Acting the part, he bowed his lowly famished head with puppy dog eyes.

"Patrick and Greg! Why aren't you helping your brother? I've told you a thousand times he is not to be out of bed, only for restroom and baths. Paul, get back in bed this instant!"

She stomped toward the TV and turned it off. Patrick and Greg protested and stared hard at the little goblin.

"Mom, this isn't fair. He knew we were watching our show and purposely asked for cereal. He could have waited. He doesn't even wake up this early." Greg huffed.

"So, he *did* ask you for help then, did he?" She was mad.

This entire episode tried everyone, and usually, injuries, bumps, and bruises were over in a few days. But the BB gun to the eye has taxed everyone and created one little monster. "Now, both of you march your butts in the kitchen and make him cereal."

She hurried back to her bedroom, and Patrick and Greg looked at Paul. He gave a sly smirk and sat in his bed, ready for his cereal.

Patrick brandished his fist, and Greg stuck his tongue out as they entered the kitchen. Paul could hear them mumbling. Paul seized his chance as soon as Virginia changed into her work clothes and returned to get her coffee.

With his famous pouting look, he tattled, "Mom, they're being mean to me."

Without hesitation, she turned to the boys. "Is this true?"

"No, he is doing this on purpose, it's like he is slaving us around, and I don't dig it!" Greg fumed.

"Well, Mr., I *don't dig it*! Who are the irresponsible young men who leave guns lying around, so people can get shot? Now, don't you back-sass me, or else you will learn to hate your Christmas break!" Storming to the coffee, she said, "When I get home, I better not hear one complaint, and you, Paul Wesley, you better behave!"

Paul sank into his bed, questioning how far he could push the limits once she left. Before he knew it, an uncontrollable urge to press the boundaries flew from his lips, "Mommy, before you leave, can I watch TV, please?" He lay on the thick, wide open, big brown eyes and, again, the puppy-dog face.

She said *yes*.

Virginia ordered Patrick to turn it on for him, and Patrick was immediately enraged.

"Don't worry, Mom, we will be nice," Patrick said, with a glance at Paul filled with impending doom.

 Paul's eyes grew wide with fear for his life. He wished she didn't have to leave.

Off to work, she drove, and the boys cleared the room. Paul noticed that no one wanted to be around him anymore and that maybe he was pushing it too far. Still, the feeling of power flowed in every fiber of his being, and he couldn't put the brakes on. He salivated for the next victim. Soon the next prey appeared, and it was Keith.

"Can you please change the channel?"

Puffy-eyed and half asleep, Keith walked right by without a glance and headed for breakfast. He poured his cereal and stared at his bowl.

Aggravated and raising his voice, Paul demanded, "Keith, will you please change the channel?"

Glancing over to the TV, Keith was expressionless. Like coffee to a grown-up, cereal was the elixir for youth.

After Keith rinsed his bowl, he changed the channel, got dressed, went outside, and didn't return. Paul sat there waiting, hearing Maureen's record player slightly through the walls. Cynthia was still in bed, and Patrick and Greg dared not come out. Paul knew they were planning his demise. Finally, having to use the bathroom, Paul got out of bed, closed the bathroom door, and locked it. Using the facilities, he kept an attentive ear.

Suddenly, as if on cue, several doors opened and closed. A stampede followed, speeding down the hallway, and the front door opened and slammed shut. Paul hurried to flush, ran to his bed, and the house was silent.

He ran to the front window; Patrick, Greg, and Keith had their guns, most likely heading to the ditches. He lowered his head and wished he could join them but knew he couldn't. He hated missing adventures.

An hour passed and then two, and nothing.

Finally, Cynthia awoke. "Good morning, Paul. How are you? Can I get you anything?" she asked, waiting and staring. Cynthia was always kind.

"No, thank you," he answered.

"Okay, you let me know if you do." Smiling, she ate her cereal, and before she went to her room, she asked him again, and he thanked her and said no.

Hot on the heels of Cynthia's kind helpfulness, the three boys returned laughing after a great time. They stepped through the front door, and Paul quickly saw his chance and screamed, "Can one of you please make me a sandwich? I'm really hungry!"

He sat back and smirked.

Patrick walked to the foot of the bed and then looked at Keith. "The next time Keith, if you were to have an accident, make sure you finish the job, so we don't have to deal with this little monster!"

They went to the kitchen, and Cynthia returned. Paul sank deep.

"Hey, Paul, do you need anything?" she asked. "I can make you a sandwich?"

"No, thanks." He quieted.

Just then, Greg came around the corner and tossed the plate on his bed. "Here is your food, your Kingship."

Cynthia turned to Paul and stared, then looked at her brothers. "Oh, I see what's going on. I offer to help, and you won't take it, so you can boss your brothers around. You are pushing it, and Mom will hear about this."

"I am not. I, I just got hungry now." He sank deeper, and he knew she saw through his sinister plan.

"Yep, sure," she sarcastically replied. "Don't lie to me. Mom will hear of this."

The brothers joined Cynthia.

Keith asked, "You mean you offered to help him, and he didn't want it? So, he waits for us to boss around? Man, Paul, you are not cool. In fact, we all can't wait to tell Mom. Is there anything else you would like?"

Patrick added, "You have become a power-hungry little idiot, and you are in big trouble."

Paul was silent and suddenly lost his appetite, not knowing Maureen was standing there the whole time.

She said, "I heard everything, Paul, and yes, it's five against one. Mom will hear from all of us when she gets home. Do you have anything you would like to say?"

With his balloon of power deflating, he stared with one eye at each angry face and realized that he had pushed too far.

"I'm sorry. I just want to go play. I want to be with you. I guess I am sick and tired of being in bed. I'm really sorry."

Feeling sympathetic for her baby brother, Maureen offered, "We can fix that, come to the table, and let's play a board game."

Cynthia and Keith joined. She pulled out Keith's new game after asking for permission. It was one of his Christmas presents.

"Yes, let's play the Ice Cube Game."

Keith went to the freezer and retrieved the small tray that held little molded ice cubes shaped like heads, complete with faces. Once popped from the tray, they fit on clever plastic feet and are capped with a plastic hat. You win if your ice cube survives the many dangerous vices, like the hot shower or salt sprinkles.

For the next few hours, Paul was ecstatic to be out of bed.

When Virginia came home, Maureen explained every detail, and Virginia sternly glared at Paul concerning his shenanigans. Maureen suggested it was time for the bed to return to his room, and their mom agreed.

The boys were excited to help rid the living room of his throne, and within a few days, all was back to normal, and the little tyrant learned his lesson and returned to being just boring ole Paul.

Chapter 17

Neighborhood Stories & Friends

What's better than the feeling of school letting out on a Friday? One thing could be the feeling of waking up early on a Saturday morning to play all day. The six kids' neighborhood was full of young and old families. There was even a rumor of a retired movie star living among them. Whether this was true or not, Virginia and the kids believed it was. But they tried to see if they could catch a glimpse of the glitzy old actress.

One Saturday morning, Keith and Paul rode their bikes up 41st street. A caregiver was walking down the road, holding a very fancy elderly woman's hand. She was dressed in a peach outfit, pants, white shoes, an elaborate matching shawl, and a fanciful tilted hat. Her warm smiling face was adorned with heavy eye makeup, long eyelashes, and bright red lipstick. Her countenance screamed, "Movie star!"

The boys thought, whoever she was, she sure looked elegant. Giddy, they waved to the believed celebrity, and she smiled and waved in return. The famed individual then carefully watched where she was stepping. This definitely played into the rumors this legendary actress was living there temporarily for health reasons. Banning was known for its dry climate, which helped many people who sought solace there for medical purposes throughout the years. The boys described to their mom what she looked like.

With total assurance, Virginia answered, "Yep, that's Gloria Swanson."

The famed actress was born in 1899 and passed in 1983. She was nominated for several awards in her long and successful career in Hollywood movies. Most notable was Sunset Boulevard in 1950.

There were many children on both streets as well. If one couldn't play, we knocked on the next door until we found one. Eventually, someone was always able to spring loose from the shackles of chores.

The neighbor girls down the street, Christi, Amy, and Sara, had a plethora of Fisher-Price sets of Little People. These toys were small round-headed, wooden figures. The Peoples fit perfectly in the little round depressions in their toy cars, tractors, swing set, and bouncing buggy accessories. The farm set had a barndoor that opened with a clever, *mooo!*

Virginia's youngest children spent untold hours sitting in the neighbor's garage on their concrete, setting up and tearing down Little People's worlds.

The neighborhood girls were always spirited with smiles and youthful play. Even their Beagle was friendly. Their father, Joe, helped the older boys with woodworking tools, creating cabinets, and just the simple function of the underlying wood trade. In the later years, their mother, Vernita, helped tutor Paul with math…she was always helpful and smiling.

Next door was Terry and Bonnie and their two children, TJ and Tesha. TJ is mentioned later on. Terry and Brenda lived next to them with their two children, Shannon and Scott. Terry took the boys under his mechanical wings and shared his wisdom with everything automotive. Next to them was the very animated Jack and his older sister Sheila.

Jack loved to push the fine line between fun and trouble. Like when Greg and Jack, hiding in a field, were shooting bottle rockets at an unsuspecting neighbor's front door. The neighbor would come out, flashlight in hand, see nothing, then head inside. Thus, another bottle rocket was launched at his door—you get the picture. All for laughs, of course.

That is just one story of many that my older brothers and Jack unleashed on the world and most likely can fill another book.

Up the street lived Valorie and Stephanie and their neighbor, Lisa. They get mentioned later. Our street always burst with kid activities.

Bike riding was the essential mode of kid transportation. The old ball-bearing skateboards or roller skates were impossible on the bumpy asphalt street. And if one tried, it would vibrate their eyeballs out of the sockets.

At the bottom of the neighborhood, there were dirt roads and fields. One area was a deep impression and a long distance across. The boys figured it was a great place to shoot bows and arrows.

"Hey, Paul?" Keith asked.

"What do you want?"

"Want me to teach you how to shoot a bow and arrow?" Keith grabbed his gear.

"Yes, that's cool! Can I bring my little bow?"

"Sure, it's just a toy, but you can bring it."

Paul jumped, put on his shoes, and off they went to the broad and deep field.

They made their way into the depression. Partway up the adjacent hill, Keith set the targets. This was the perfect placement for safety if a stray decided to ricochet.

"Okay, here's my rules. I will need to shoot several times, and you will go get them. You have to earn the right to learn how to shoot."

Paul stared and already suspected foul play. "You mean I'm your slave?"

"No, fathead, that's not what I'm doing. You want to learn or what?" Keith fumed, knowing his plan was very transparent.

"All right then!" Paul steamed back.

As arrow after arrow was expelled, Paul made trip after trip, just like a ball-boy in a major tennis rally. Boredom quickly set in as Keith was clearly on the fun end of the stick. While clutching his little bow, Paul walked back and forth, pretending to shoot at the enemy pouring over the rise.

After eliminating his imaginary enemy more times than he could count, Paul stopped. Annoyed, he said, "Hey, you lied to me. That's it. You're never gunna let me shoot your bow. You're a liar! I'm going home and telling Mom."

Paul threw the arrows down at Keith's feet.

"Don't tattle on me, you little fathead! I was just going to start teaching you how to shoot."

"Liar!" Paul stood there, staring.

"This is my last round, I promise." Keith shot another round, and Paul began to walk toward home.

"Wait, here's my plan. You take your toy bow and shoot the arrow back my way. Don't worry, that cheap toy isn't strong enough to reach me. So, you stay on that side, and I will stay on this side. Got it? This way, I can watch and see how good a shot you are."

Paul looked at Keith, mulled over the idea, and nodded. Walking to the hill again to retrieve the arrows, he saw one resting toward the top. Keith was sitting in his tyrannical spot, awaiting the incoming arrows so he could retrieve them.

Paul decided to reach the farthest first. He stood on top of the hill and set his feet. Mimicking how his brother shot, he set the arrow, looked down, and across where Keith sat watching. Raising his bow to gauge the distance, he fired, *twang!* Off the arrow went.

Keith sat calmly watching the high, straight shot, but then a sudden and sheer panic set in. He quickly realized that his arrow was flying down directly at him. He tried to sit up quickly, watching it soar straight at his body. He dodged right, left, right again, then finally leaped to the left, rolling on the sticker-covered ground and thud.

The arrow stuck precisely where he was sitting, wiggling slightly from the landing. Paul smiled and felt that no more practice was needed and walked home. The session was over.

To the west of the neighborhood, bordered by Omar, Wilson, and Ramsey streets, were many trails. The endless dirt paths for bike riding called the kids for daily adventure.

There was a single wash splitting the trails down the middle. Jumps and hills were abundant, and this giant playground used up most hours of play. Every type of trail one could imagine was there. Dune buggies, Jeeps, trucks, and motorcycles used this area for fun, and it was basically in their backyard. Also, it was the quickest place to reach when the wild called them to hunt. Many days shooting BB guns were spent, which rendered the ground almost copper-like.

South of the trails was known as the old golf course. The few remnants were an old wooden bridge covered in overgrowth, spanning the wash, and a left-over sign frame. On the back corner of the trails was a large grove of eucalyptus. Rumors were that the railroad company planted and plotted them all over Banning. The wood was supposed to be for making ties for railroad tracks. Apparently, the wood was not suited for the project, so the abandoned groves remained. The perfectly lined trees at night made for spooky play.

One day, Paul and a neighbor friend TJ were hiking through the grove, and they spotted what appeared to be an abandoned dune buggy. Its old silver frame looked intact, and all tires were sound. This open-air buggy shot dreams through their minds at a rapid pace. The lone rollbar over the driver's seat looked cool.

"Wow, I wonder who left this here, let's get in," Paul said as he jumped into the pilot's seat and TJ in the other.

There was a lone button on the dash frame, and Paul grinned. He looked at TJ and pushed it in. The quiet grove lit up with the sound of a roaring VW motor.

To their surprise, the buggy was in gear, something the boys knew nothing about. They couldn't even reach the brake pedals. The buggy lurched forward when he held the starter button. Paul panicked as he tried to reach the brake.

He didn't think to let go of the starter button. The engine cranked until a tree got in the way. Both were shot forward, crashing into the dash. The motor stalled, and the dust cleared. The bruised boys felt suddenly scared. Peeling themselves out, they fled the crash scene. Once they realized they were running away from no one, they slowed their pace. The boys, wide-eyed, looked at each other and burst into laughter.

"Let's go tell my brothers," Paul said as he noticed his arm was wet. He looked down and found, of course, it was blood. He had a minor gash on his right arm. "Man, my mom doesn't need to know about this. Can I wash it at your house?"

TJ nodded as they ran back to their home. Dousing the wound using his front garden hose, Paul cleaned it the best he could. He did not want his mother to see yet another injury.

Entering the home, Paul shouted, "Patrick! There's a dune buggy at the trails, and it works. Someone left it there!"

"You're pulling my leg, a real one?" Patrick jumped up from his TV show.

"Yes, and it even starts," Paul stated.

TJ nodded eagerly behind him.

"Far out! Wait, did you start it? Did you drive it?" Patrick's smile quickly faded.

Feeling like a scared car thief, Paul hesitated and looked around, and their mom wasn't in the room. Paul nodded and showed him his wound.

Patrick said, "That's cool. Where's the buggy?"

With adrenaline pumping through him, Paul and TJ led his brothers to the grove.

Patrick and Greg followed as they brought them to the car, and the older boys jumped in and fired it up. Grinding the gears, they blew through the grove, and off they went. The joy ride of joy rides was complete.

Paul and TJ looked on with excitement. A nagging feeling lingered that the buggy was stolen and dumped there. After the thrill was over, they returned it. Rumors were that Patrick's friend took it home to salvage it, but the motor caught fire, so he dumped it back in the grove. The boys were bummed to notice that the buggy was gone by that weekend.

The foothills were north of their house, and the Banning Bench was northeast. A dead-end street called Mountain Ave led up to the base of the foothills, where what the kids called the "rich neighborhood." These homes were large and beautiful. The road was long and had a semi-steep grade, then tapered level in the last stretch by a small church. It was a long road with a kink in it halfway up.

"I'm going to try it," Greg said as he grabbed his skateboard. "You guys want to go?"

Keith and Paul nodded because they wanted to see their brother wipe out.

Walking up the long road on a bright Saturday afternoon, Greg tucked his board under his arm as he bragged how the ride would be easy. There were no elbow pads, knee pads, or helmets in those days, just pure guts. Now, the old-school skateboards were narrow, and the wheels not the highest technology like today's boards. Plus, there was untested physics involved. A tiny and narrow board under a large and tall body, nothing could go wrong with that…right?

"I don't know Greg, you're gunna wipe out," Keith said as he looked at the grade.

"Are you scared?" Paul asked.

"No way, I'm going for it. I ain't no sissy."

The younger halted below the kink in the road as Greg kept his long walk up until he turned. Wasting no time, he set the board and slowly stepped on.

Watching in disbelief, the young brothers both thought, *Cool!*

Greg was poised, in control, and quickly approaching as he steamed down the hill. Keith and Paul were amazed as he swiftly passed their position, watching in awe as the rocket skater jetted by. But something began to go horribly wrong.

The skater's sound barrier shattered, and Greg looked down under his unsuspecting feet as an uncontrollable speed wobble began. This wasn't any old tremor; it was catastrophic. Within seconds, Greg was forced to jettison the death trap. He may have taken one or two controlled steps before his body was thrown into the asphalt. He thrashed about while careening off the road into the tumbleweeds and bullhead stickers.

Strangely, the lone board continually rolled straight down the road as if all was well. The boys ran to the discarded passenger to see his fate. Reaching his carcass, they thought of how they would have to explain his death to their mom, but Greg groaned and sprang up. Blood dripped from every location through his torn shirt and pants, and stickers abounded.

"Stupid board!" he yelled. "I need to tighten the trucks as best I can. They're too loose."

While walking home, Greg bragged about how fun it was and how he would defeat the monstrous hill. The younger thought he was brave, and they dug it.

An hour passed, and Greg found his brothers. "You want to watch again? I tightened the trucks, and I'm good to go."

Keith and Paul looked at each other and thought for sure the end of Greg was near. But who wouldn't pass up another good wipeout?

Poised again, watching their wounded brother ascend, he stepped on the board, and off he went. Flying by at a higher speed, the board was smooth and straight. Reaching critical mass, the boys were sure he had broken the real sound barrier as he screamed by his previous crash site. This time, he cut the wind with fast speed, and down to the bottom he went, slowing to a stop.

"Keith, that was so cool! Greg's like a stuntman," Paul said.

Keith's smile was from ear to ear. "Let's borrow his board. It's our turn to try!"

Thus, started the great Mountain Avenue skate-run, where many cuts and bruises were formed and an embedded sheen of skin that would forever be etched in the pavement.

Speaking of Mountain Avenue, the same trio endeavored to climb the foothills one summer night. These same hills held the old famed, early 1970's Petty plane crash site. It was a hike to reach the somber and molten wreckage, but worth it.

After leaping the barbed wire fence, they followed a small wash, then headed for the power pole road. Several tall towers were planted over the hills, bringing electricity for miles. What was the trio to do? Well, climb them, of course. Greg led the charge.

"Check out how easy this is." He shimmied up like nothing, and as soon as he did, a coyote let out a yelp that could have awakened the dead.

Keith followed, and then Paul. The good news was that Greg looked out for their safety and explained, "Never ever climb up to the top of the towers," he said, pointing straight up. "You'll be cooked. Tens of thousands of volts will fry you like an electric chair."

Laughing, the boys could hear the current zapping through the lines but could barely see them since it was pitch black.

Dangling on the steel, the brothers joked and teased until a lone siren echoed in the valley in the distance. Suddenly, one howl of a coyote, then two, then more. The next thing they knew, a pack of those scoundrels swirled directly below the tower. Paul swore it was a hundred, but Greg comforted his exaggerations by confirming only twenty or so.

As the siren drew closer, the mongrels turned up the barking and howling volume, and soon, Greg dipped down, antagonizing them. Keith and Paul clutched the tower. Greg continued yelling at the pack and then did the unthinkable.

"Come on, you stupid coyotes, lookout, I'm gunna get you!"

He leaped off the tower, landed in the middle of the scraggly dogs, and they scattered like shrieks of lightning. Within a second, the mutts vaporized into the shadows. Greg laughed as the two chickens tried focusing on his position through the blackness.

From the darkness, they heard their brother say, "See you later."

He quickly walked down the road, and Keith and Paul stared in fright at what lurked in the shadows. Without a thought, they scrambled down lickety-split and sprinted in the dead of night after Greg.

When they caught him, he said, "What took you so long, you bunch of sissies!"

Chapter 18

Hard Decision

After the new year rang in 1974, the President of the United States was forced to resign. Muhammad Ali returned to boxing and knocked out George Foremen in the eighth round to reclaim his heavyweight title. The eight-hundred-mile Alaskan pipeline began, and gas was forty-two cents a gallon. IRA terrorist bombings were being planned in Britain, and Henry Kissinger convinced Syria to a cease-fire with Israel in the Golan Heights.

With February rolling around, spring in Southern California was always in the air. A blanket of weeds popped up throughout the front yard, and Virginia was determined to get the troops out to start pulling.

On a Friday night, the phone rang, and it was Charlie.

"Hello Virginia, how are you and the kids?"

Happy yet terrified to hear his voice, she paused and looked down, taking a deep breath. "We are doing good. How are you?"

"I'm good, and I have something for you."

Say no, Virginia. Don't take what he's offering. You don't deserve it. "What is it?" she asked nervously.

"My neighbor pulled up his entire yard, and I have a truck full of sod, so we can get your lawn going."

Her heart sank at his thoughtfulness. That was what she liked about Charlie. He was always a step ahead, wanting to meet her needs. And he seemed to know the things she loved, not trinkets or cheap gifts. The sod would be enjoyable to look at and for the kids to play on.

Charlie had the talent to fix things that most people would end up paying someone to repair. She knew, in her mind, that here was a man who listened. He listened to her needs and wanted to please and bless her with no demands. He was genuinely a kind man.

She melted at the offer and said, "Charlie, that's wonderful. I'll take it. Can I pick it up somewhere?" Knowing full well, she had no means.

"I would like to bring it in the morning if that's okay. It is sort of, well, all in the back of my pickup truck. I will have the kids help, and I presume some weeds need to be pulled."

"Thank you, Charlie, there are weeds, and it was my plan to have them pulled tomorrow. So, this is perfect timing. See you in the morning. I'll have coffee ready."

Hanging up the phone, she sighed. *You sure aren't making this easy, are you?*

~

The next morning, Virginia opened her eyes, and the light of the day was dawning. She stumbled to get dressed and washed her face while the kids were still sleeping. She headed to the kitchen, filled the pot full, scooped the coffee into the percolator, and brewing Folgers ruled the air.

She began her self-rebuke by sharpening her art of conversation with herself while cleaning the kitchen.

"Virginia, today is the day. You need to be strong and let him know that it won't work between you two…no matter how much you like him." A long sigh came next, and she wavered. "But he would be an excellent father."

Her stomach twisted in knots. "How many times do I remind you that you're not even divorced…do you want to open that can of worms?" Sighing deeply again, she went to the living room curtains. Opening them wide, she jumped and yelled, "Ah!"

Startled, she saw it was Charlie, under the window, offloading the massive load of sod quietly in the cool before the sun. Virginia pointed at him, and he laughed because he once again had frightened her. Her guard suddenly melted like butter at his dedication and love for hard work.

Opening the front door, she said, "Charlie, you will be the one to give me a heart attack!"

"I'm sorry, Virginia. Of course, you have already heard that several times, haven't you?" He laughed.

"Come in. You want a cup of coffee?"

"Sure, thought you'd never ask. Since I have been out here alone, working for hours?"

Virginia stopped. "No, you're kidding, right?" she said, half believing him.

"Of course, I just got here." He smiled.

She opened the dining room curtain, and the sun was now peeking, and he began to run by the game plan for the planting, but her thoughts strongly blanked him out.

Staring into his eyes, she imagined what it would be like to be married to him—wondering if he would stick around and be a good father to the kids. Wondering if he would love her for who she was.

Virginia was entranced by his wavy brown hair and a thick mustache. *He is handsome, though.*

"Virginia, Virginia?" He paused.

Snapping out of her spell and embarrassed, her cheeks flushed as she flippantly said, "Yes." *Yes, yes, to what? What did he ask?*

Thankfully, Charlie seemed to catch on as he asked, "Did you hear a word I said?"

"No." She laughed. "I was thinking of…when I should wake the kids?" Her quick excuse seemed to work.

"You said yes, to what? I didn't ask a question. But I can reform my statement into a question, I guess." He sipped his coffee.

"I'm sorry, it's early, and I haven't had my coffee yet."

They both chuckled.

"I said. It looks like we don't have enough sod, but this type of grass will spread. So, we can place the grass anywhere you want. Do you have a favorite spot where you sit and look at your yard?

Her next words came before she could stop them, "Thanks for thinking of me. That's sweet."

Once again, the knots tightened in her stomach. *Virginia! Stop it!*

She quickly changed the conversation back on track. "Go ahead and start the grass under the front window. I think it will look nicer there." Rising and looking out, she said, "Would you like a few eggs and bacon?"

"Yes, please, you're the best cook ever." He held a gentle stare into her eyes longer than usual, making her blush.

"I'll wake the boys, so they can get to helping. I'll throw in pancakes as well. You'll all earn a hearty breakfast."

"Ah, Virginia, you are the kindest and most thoughtful person I know. Thank you." Charlie stood, drained his cup, and headed for the sink to wash it.

"Here, just set it down. You don't have to wash your dishes. I'll do that for you."

Reaching for the cup, she unintentionally grabbed his hand and found herself holding it for a moment. A rush of emotions swelled, followed once again by embarrassment.

Stumbling over her words, she said, "You, I will, I will wash your hand for you, I mean, dish." *Good grief, Virginia!*

Charlie could tell she was embarrassed. "I'm sorry, I do all my own dishes. You know why?"

"Because you live alone?"

"Nope, Hildegard, my lovely golden retriever, finally put his paw down and said he refuses to wash them anymore."

Laughing, he went outside.

She chuckled and shook her head as he left. She found him to be so kind and funny, to boot. Tears welled as her heart felt crushed. There was no more putting off the conversation that needed to happen. *I can't be with him, even though I want to so badly. He is, in my definition, perfect. Perfect for my kids. But I am not divorced, and it is against my religion. What would the church think if I married him? He's so nice, but I don't deserve him. He needs a young, pretty wife, not me. I want a good man like him, but, but...*

"Morning, Mom," Patrick said as Greg, Keith, and Paul, followed.

"Oh, I was going to wake you," she said, turning to hide her tearful eyes. "Thank you, boys. It's going to be a busy day today. Charlie is already outside. Go help him, and breakfast will be ready soon. I want full stomachs for the hard-working kids."

Excited, Greg said as he ran for his shoes, "Charlie is already here? Cool!"

The boys were thrilled and expressed it, and Virginia's heart dropped even lower, knowing how much Charlie meant to them. *I wish I can open my heart to my children and tell them what I am going through. I don't want to crush them. I want them to have a good man in their life besides John Wayne.*

The kids flew out the door, and the sod off-loading and planting began. Charlie masterfully had the boys working together as an excellent running orchestra.

Between flipping pancakes and stirring eggs, she occasionally glanced out the window at Charlie, seeing him laughing and instructing the boys. Every once in a while, she caught herself staring a little too long and quickly looked away. Her heart was mangled at what decision to make, knowing her youth wasn't hanging around, knowing it wouldn't be easy to find such a good man.

Anger boiled as past thoughts invaded her daydreaming. Quick glimpses of her tough road that started over eight years ago seemed to suddenly stifle any emotions or feelings she had for Charlie. *God, God, I feel as if it was all my fault. I don't want the kids to be hurt anymore. If it was me who ruined the last marriage, once he gets to know me, he will probably leave me to. I couldn't stomach it...it would kill me.*

The failed marriage was, of course, no fault of her own. She did everything she could to save it. But when her husband left her and the kids with nothing but a hand wave through a hospital window, she couldn't help but question if it was something she did.

Eyes soaking again, she snapped out of it and concentrated hard on completing breakfast.

Maureen and Cynthia joined to help set the hearty feast on the table, and soon, the entire troops washed up and sat down.

"We will say grace," Virginia insisted.

They all bowed their heads, and the wafting of bacon smell caused some of their eyes to stay open.

Charlie's hands were folded and his head down as the kids felt he was comfortable with it. After a strong "Amen," they dove in and devoured the delightful spread.

Soon, they were back in the hot sun, but the troops worked feverishly under Charlie's command. By lunch, the sod was in place and being watered.

Maureen entered the house and washed up, helping with lunch, and this time the food was brought outside, and everyone ate at their leisure. All were enjoying the new look of the yard, which was now green. Gone were the familiar dirt and weeds.

The work was now hard as yawns and dreams of napping entered a few of the boys' minds. However, no one would dare miss working with Charlie.

They plucked weeds, and to Virginia's delight, the yard radiated beauty. With the green grass, and the weeds gone, she could now see where she could plant roses.

The boys sprayed down the concrete and, of course, each other. It was now getting close to dinner time, and all was complete, cleaned, and tools put away.

Charlie knew how to plan, implement, and complete a job. Virginia was beyond thrilled, and the children were still full of energy.

"Charlie, this is wonderful."

Cynthia yelled, "Mom, you mean far out!"

Laughing, Virginia replied, "Okay, this is…far out!"

The kids didn't want Charlie to leave, so Virginia struggled to invite him for dinner. *Don't let him think you're falling for him. You got to keep your distance.*

Charlie hung around waiting for an invite, but Charlie, being Charlie, was even thoughtful when he detected tension in the air. He smiled and said, "Kids, I have to be going."

The gang protested and offered to go home with him. They loved his old house and his incredibly friendly dog.

"Maybe I can come back soon if I am invited this time." He looked at Virginia with a half-smile, sensing a struggle.

Cynthia yelled, "Mom, Easter is around the corner. Can Charlie join us for Easter dinner?"

The chorus joined in with the same song as some hopped in excitement. Something elevated in Virginia's heart as if this was the springboard of their future or the dividing road that would stop this idea of her and Charlie becoming a couple.

She couldn't control the words that flew from her heart. "No! I am sorry, we will only be having Easter with family."

A stillness settled over everyone as Charlie's face dropped, and everyone could read his expression, which hurt.

A long pause hung coldly, and Charlie quickly warmed as he cleared his throat and smiled. Pain riddled his eyes, and Virginia was ready to explode into tears. She was prepared to take back everything she had just said and leap into his arms to be held by someone who cared, but she fought back, knowing the pain she had just caused. So, she stood her confusing ground.

"Kids," Charlie said. "It has been a thrill and a joy working with you. You boys promise to work this hard your whole life, and you will do great things."

The younger kids beamed and couldn't wait to spend more time with him. The older kids felt a shift that maybe something drastic happened and not for anything good. Cynthia felt a rush of guilt, as if it was her fault.

Charlie spoke again. "Virginia, thank you for everything. Thanks for letting me help you these last few years. You have wonderful kids, and you are doing a great job. If you ever need anything…" He paused as he began to fight back the tears. "Ah, if you need anything, please...I'm only a phone call away."

Virginia felt crushed. A deep void pained her broken heart as if she just threw a great opportunity away.

Charlie gave each kid a friendly and affectionate smile, and then a long warm smile to Virginia. Somehow, he knew her real struggle.

He glanced over the yard work as the visible tears welled and said, "You all take care now. It's been wonderful."

Charlie dropped his head, and his forced smile faded as he got in his truck. Backing out, the younger kids were bouncing with goodbyes, as the older ones had a strange feeling that he might not be coming back. Slowly driving up the street, he waved and was gone.

Tears quickly welled in Virginia's eyes, and pain and doubt filled her heart. *Relationships are so hard. Why is this hard? Why is it so darn painful?*

Her heart felt so many things at once. First, she felt guilty that she had broken his heart. Second, she was worried that she had made a horrible decision, and third, she felt shattered that she had lost someone she truly cared about.

Virginia couldn't muster the courage to address the kids. Her hands moved to hide her face as she turned and headed for the front door. She felt sick in her stomach.

She swiftly moved to her bathroom, locked the door, and turned on the sink. Sitting on the edge of the tub, she wept. She sobbed to the point of feeling faint. It was like a weight of bricks on her chest, making her gasp for air between each sob. The cries were not just for Charlie, although many tears were for their friendship and the pain of having to end it. But much of the sobbing was about life, her situation, and her lack of trust—also, fears of entering another relationship only to end in ruin. *What about my dreams of love and just wanting a broad-shouldered man to hold me tight?*

The feel of a warm hug, and words of kindness, were fading quickly with each year. Finally, this dark cloud of no divorce in sight felt like knives beginning to carve ulcers in her stomach.

Sliding down in heart-wrenching pain on the cold floor, Virginia buried her face in a towel to soak up all her tears. She curled up, crying harder than she ever had before.

The kids had the sense to leave Mom alone, and after Maureen listened quietly by the bathroom door, she heard the endless water running and knew to walk away. Heading to the kitchen, she noticed that dinner was started and continued to finish.

Maureen asked her brothers and sister to wash up and sit down, and they obeyed, much to her surprise, and gathered around the table.

Virginia appeared in the kitchen, quiet and refreshed. "Maureen, thank you for helping. It's very kind."

Now joining her family, Virginia said, "Let's all say grace. Bless us, oh Lord, for these thy gifts, which we are about to receive, through Thy bounty, through Christ, our Lord. In the name of the Father, the Son, and the Holy Spirit, amen."

Chapter 19

Love is Hard

Virginia's next few weeks forced her down a dark and hard road of the future. She often wondered what tomorrow would hold, love or loneliness.

Deep scars and hurtful wounds seemed to bleed again. Massive doubts and confused thoughts about Virginia's marriage separation made her think she was at fault again. Guilt smothered because she was technically still married by the state.

Trying to figure out how to bring her marriage to an end made her sick. Many prayers were voiced, which brought her comfort. But one thing that seemed to hurt was the vision of the future. Though she still had her children, she often felt a great sense of loneliness. *Will I ever marry again?*

Each week of stress seemed to strip away years of her life. Virginia hoped to see her children grow and to see grandkids. But was it to be a road of being alone? Thoughts like this kept her up at night, all alone in her single bed.

One night, staring at the ceiling, she was thinking of her mom, and quickly her mind swept to the vague memories of her father, who passed away when she was sixteen. *Grandma made it all these years alone, and she's content. Dad, what would my life have been like if you were still alive?*

His encouragement, laughter, and his gripping hugs seemed so long ago. Thinking hard of the few recollections, a sudden flash of her childhood arose when she was seven years old.

"Virginia!" Father hollered, wearing a huge smile. "Come here. Let me wrap my arms around you."

Her curly blonde hair bounced as Virginia ran to him. "Yes, Papa?"

"My leave is over, and I have to go back to work. The Big E's calling."

"But why, and what's a biggie calling?"

"My ship, the USS Enterprise, we call her the Big E. And it's my job to take care of her. Just like your mother will take care of you on this ship, the house. Hey, I'll be in Hawaii. I will send you a postcard, and be sure to write to me." Picking her up, he kissed her cheek and embraced her one more time. "Please, I need all of your prayers you can send my way, my little V. Do you promise?"

Giggling, she said, "Yes, I promise."

"Ah, that's my girl. I love you, Virginia."

"I love you too and will miss you." She paused, staring with sad eyes. "I wish you didn't have to go," she said.

He sat her down gently, placing his hands on her shoulders. "I know. I wish I didn't either, but I have to. And remember, this isn't goodbye, but see you later." He winked and stood up.

He flung his duffle bag over his shoulder and kissed Frankie goodbye. Stepping out into the cab, he waved. Frankie was holding her infant, Joyce, standing next to Virginia and two older brothers, Lloyd and Stan. Each of them waved back.

The taxi door closed, and he drove away to the naval yard.

Months passed, and December began, and Virginia was excited for Christmas. She hoped to spend it with her father and see his eyes widen when he opened her present. Upstairs, after rummaging through the material bag, Virginia was hand-making him a gift. She had sewn him a new handkerchief.

Her stomach growled suddenly, knowing it was time to take a break. The drifting aroma of baking lured her down into the kitchen,

She asked, "What smells so good?"

Frankie was wearing a white apron with embroidered flowers on the front. "I am making muffins for supper. Will you help me? I need you to put away the flour."

Virginia nodded and began to help her mom when she said, "I miss Papa."

Bending down, her mom said, "And rightly so. We all do. But absence makes the heart grow fonder."

"What's that mean?"

"You are so inquisitive." Pulling the first batch from the oven, she said, "Come here."

Frankie set a warm muffin in front of Virginia and poured a glass of milk. "Here now, this will help your hunger until supper."

"Did you ever miss your papa?" Virginia asked, taking a large bite of her treat. She stared.

"Well, I guess you're old enough to know. My father left when I was very, very young. You see, he wanted a son but had me instead." She sat next to Virginia and continued, "This was in 1908. He was a drunkard and didn't love us. So, he left. Now, my mother had a hard go of it, so when I was three, I was sent to Arkansas to live with my grandma and grandpa, the Knowles. They were sharecroppers. Meaning they would give food for food. He had four hundred acres of sugarcane.

"They loved me, and I loved them. Why grandpa even built me my own room. But know this, they put us to work really young. I used to ride the old mule, Bessie. She turned the grinder. Sugar cane went in the top, and the mill would grind it down with every circle. You see," she used her hands to paint the motion, "round and round, I would go, and the mill would turn and grind the cane down, so grandpa could make his sugar. And it was sweet as you," she said as she bounced one of Virginia's curls.

Virginia laughed. "Sounds like fun!"

"Those were good times. So, you asked me if I missed my father. The answer is no. I hardly knew him. But I do miss grandma and grandpa. Oh, Virginia, I pray to God Almighty, and he helps my heart feel better. You miss your papa because you love him, and that's a good thing. You and I will pray for him and write to him often. Okay?"

"Okay. I promised Papa I would." She finished her muffin and gulped down the milk.

"When we have time, I will tell you how you are related to the famous frontiersman, Daniel Boone," Frankie said.

Virginia looked puzzled. "Papa told me about him before. He lived a long time ago."

"Yes, he did."

They heard a sudden pounding on the door.

Their front door burst open, and Martha, their friendly neighbor, yelled, "Can you believe it? Are you listening to the radio?" Wasting no time, she waved for Frankie to follow. "Frankie, come listen to the broadcast, hurry!"

Grabbing Virginia's hand and scooping up Joyce, they hurried down the sidewalk next door as Martha's family waved them in. Not all households could afford a radio, Frankie owned one, but it was turned off.

This commotion had to be severe enough to be alerted like this. Up the porch stairs and through the front door, they went. A tall wooden radio stood in the center of the living room against the wall. A white doily rested on top with a small clear vase displaying a single red rose. Martha's son feverishly was turning the dial with his right hand, twisting it ever so slightly; the announcer's voice was quickly clear.

"President Roosevelt has just announced the Japanese have attacked Pearl Harbor, Hawaii, by air. The attack also was made on all naval and military activities on the principal island of Oahu. We take you now to Washington."

Virginia looked at her mother and saw her face had lost all color.

"Sit down, Frankie. I'm sure Joe is okay." Martha led her to the sofa.

The air seemed to withdraw from the room as everyone stopped and stared at the continuing voice. *War, what does this mean?* Virginia wondered.

Since she was only seven years old, she thought, *why are the grownups so worried?*

The words from the wooden box ended. Frankie thanked her neighbors, and quietly, they walked home.

Virginia stared up at her mom's countenance, which was long and silent. When they entered their home, Frankie explained to her sons what this might mean. It escaped Virginia, but she understood that she might not see her papa for a long time. Her heart began to sadden.

Frankie was unusually quiet in the kitchen, with no humming or singing. She was boiling water for tea. Virginia stared around the corner, feeling scared.

Watching her mom stir her drink, she had to ask, "Momma, is papa going to be home for Christmas?"

Frankie snapped from her daze and gave a half smile. "Follow me, my dear, and sit next to me."

She led her to the living room couch, and they sat. There was a long pause before her mother said, "The truth is always best. And, that truth is…he may not be. But we will write Papa many letters, and make sure you pray every day for him. War is a dangerous business. He will need God with him every moment. Can you promise to pray and write those letters?"

Virginia nodded, but her stomach dropped at the news. She thought of the Christmas present she had made for him. Wrestling with the thought of papa not being around for Christmas seemed unreal, but something inside her drew strength from her mother.

Frankie's strength seemed unusually strong in the way of her faith in God. She would pray with the kids, say grace over every meal, and attend Sunday church. Virginia loved this about her mom. She always seemed to be in control. A solid pillar that wouldn't and couldn't fall, even with no news of how Papa was. Was he dead or alive? Frankie knew in her heart he was alive.

That evening Frankie put Joyce in the crib, and Virginia and the boys gathered feverishly around their radio for any morsel of news. However, little news was shared that night.

The next morning, they all woke early and gathered around the radio again. Frankie, however, went straight to the kitchen to prepare breakfast.

Virginia got up to help her. Lloyd and Stan stayed back and listened anxiously. Lloyd suddenly announced the President was going to speak, so they gathered around again, waiting eagerly for any news. Through static and fuzziness, the president's voice rang out.

"*Mr. Vice President, Members of the Senate, Yesterday, December 7th, 1941...a date which will live in infamy...the United States of America was suddenly and deliberately attacked by naval and air forces of the Empire of Japan.*"

The boys stared at each other like never before, asking what all that meant. "Is the war coming here? Will the enemy come running down our street?"

The nation paused as the president gave the grim news. He continued, "*The United States was at peace with that nation and...*"

As the speech continued, the children faded a bit until they heard anything mentioning Hawaii. Quickly cueing in again, the president said, "*It will be recorded that the distance of Hawaii from Japan makes it obvious that the attack was deliberately planned many days or even weeks ago. During the intervening time, the Japanese government has deliberately sought to deceive the United States by false statements and expressions of hope for continued peace.*"

It was a shock to believe that this was really happening. It was hard to imagine that war was upon the United States.

Frankie held her chest.

"*The attack on the Hawaiian Islands has caused severe damage to American naval and military forces.*"

At this news, Frankie gasped. She stood with her right hand over her mouth and headed to the front window. She drew the curtain back with an unsteady hand and stared out.

The boys looked worried, and Virginia was still confused.

The president continued, "*I regret to tell you that very many American lives have been lost.*"

Frankie quickly turned to her children and said, "Papa's all right, he's all right, pray for him and his fellow sailors. He's all right." Her voice quivered, and her eyes were full of tears.

The kids had never seen their mom this way. They quickly learned how serious and dangerous this news was.

The speech concluded, "*Yesterday, the Japanese government also launched an attack against Malaya. Last night, Japanese forces attacked Hong Kong. Last night, Japanese forces attacked Guam. Last night, Japanese forces attacked the Philippine Islands. Last night, the Japanese attacked Wake Island. And this morning, the Japanese attacked Midway Island.*" The stares were now distant and quiet. "*With confidence in our armed forces, with the unbounded determination of our people, we will gain the inevitable triumph—so help us, God. I ask that Congress declare that since the unprovoked and dastardly attack by Japan on Sunday, December 7th, 1941, a state of war has existed between the United States and the Japanese empire.*"

Frankie wiped her eyes and cleared her throat. "Boys, turn it off. It appears Papa is in this for the long haul. I want you to know he is okay; I know it. The navy has a fight on its hands. Start praying for the United States to win, so Joe can come home."

The boys nodded and very quietly turned the radio off.

The best thing for them was to go about their day as usual and try not to think about what was happening. Although, that proved difficult. The boys headed outside and took to their chores.

Virginia's heart ached. She loved her father so much. She felt aloneness started to open up, which she didn't like. No, she didn't like it at all.

Standing up and looking out the front window toward the west, she tried imagining Papa on a great ship with danger all around.

She made the sign of the cross and prayed aloud, "Lord Jesus in Heaven, please be with Papa, be with him today, and tomorrow, and forever. Help him not to get hurt, and please help his friends, his sailor friends, to be okay too. Thank you, Jesus. I ask, in the name of the Father, Son, and Holy Ghost, amen."

When her prayer ended, she felt a gentle hand rest on her shoulder. She looked to see her mom staring down at her. She gave her a soft smile, and Virginia knew these next months would be difficult for them. She became incredibly thankful for such a strong mother and hoped that when she was a mom, her kids would think the same thing. For a moment, they both stared out the window together.

Virginia rustled in her bed, and her eyes opened slowly from her sleep. She rolled over to see Cynthia and wondered what day it was. She finally realized it was the day before Easter.

Laying her head back, thinking of those days with her father so long ago, she smiled slightly. *I sure miss his voice.*

She sighed as she drew her weary body out of bed.

Unfortunately, that morning, her thoughts kept steering toward Charlie, as they often did since she let him go. He was a wonderful and true gentleman that any woman would want to marry. Several temptations overcame her to pick up the phone and apologize. There was still time, and Easter was the next day. She knew he would be alone.

Playing scenario's out over and over made Virginia's head spin. She was so caught up in the thought of reaching out that she even dialed the rotary to the last number and was holding it.

"No, Virginia, let it go." She slammed the phone down and walked away. *Stop doing this!*

Stepping outside, she looked at the new sod and thought of excuses she could make to call him back and, maybe, make it seem like she wasn't interested. *Perhaps we could just have small talk, Virginia, you know, just a little chit-chat?*

She shook her head and rolled her eyes at her foolish thoughts. She turned and headed indoors. She went to the kitchen, opened her cabinet, and reached for the pancake mix. *I just don't want to be alone for the rest of my life.*

Looking beyond the store of goods, she found a bottle of Gin she had forgotten about. Staring hard at it, she reprimanded herself, *Virginia, that is the last thing you need!*

With the kids still in bed, she unscrewed the cap and smelled it. She then pushed it back into the back and paused. Slowly, she reached for it and conveniently placed it for an easy grab higher in a smaller cabinet. *No, Virginia, no!*

Virginia made coffee and began the pancake factory for the troops. She wanted to bless them with another hardy breakfast for their big Easter weekend. The kids would dye eggs, and the older ones would hide them.

She thought of her children's future and the long road they had traveled. Then the tremendous and unforeseen distances that were still in front of them.

Virginia poured coffee and stepped outside again as the sun began to rise. Staring at the surrounding mountains, she thought of how hard love was, then about her mom's toughness of being single and how content and secure she had been her entire life. She sighed. *God, I have six children that need me, and frankly, I need them. Whatever the road, I am content. I will…learn to be content with Your help. Love is hard and hurtful; I just don't know if I can go through that again. Truthfully, I don't want to go through that again. Please guide me and be with Charlie. He is a good man who deserves a good woman.*

She reached down and picked up the morning paper, then went inside. Setting the stack of hotcakes on the table, some of the kids began to wake up. She opened the paper to the cartoons section, known as the funnies, started to read them, and managed to have a giggle or two. She shared the strips with the kids and sat back, enjoying their laughter.

Later that evening, while the kids were outside playing, she opened the cabinet and, again, stared at the bottle of gin. Grabbing it, she quickly took two huge gulps and gasped. A burn raced down her throat, and she capped it.

Virginia looked around, paused, then opened the bottle again and fired down one more large swig. She gasped at the equivalent of inhaling a full glass of gin in seconds, her head swirled, and her heart ached. Her internal battle began. *Don't start this, Virginia. It's the last thing you need.*

But I deserve it. I've gone through so much. Besides, one drink won't hurt you.

An inner struggle awoke, one she felt gripped her harder than anything else, and a troublesome pathway opened wide in front of her. One she would not think in a million years she would veer onto. Her insides screamed, *I don't care anymore. I can have a drink whenever I want to have a drink.*

Sitting down, she opened her paper and couldn't focus. Her eyes stared back at the cabinet where the gin sat. With her head spinning, she looked up as the children ran by her front window. Fear suddenly seized her. *What am I doing? I can't go down this road, it's too dark and unknown, and it never ends well. God in Heaven…please forgive me and help me!*

The End

Thanks for reading. This story concludes in, Single Mom, Six Kids, & a Piano ...The Later Years.

Made in the USA
Monee, IL
09 January 2025

76400839R00115